The
Village School

The autumn ritual of conker-cracking at Southrop School

The Village School

JUNE R. LEWIS

ROBERT HALE · LONDON

First published in Great Britain 1989

Robert Hale Limited
Clerkenwell House
Clerkenwell Green
London EC1R 0HT

British Library Cataloguing in Publication Data

Lewis, June R. (June Rosemarie)
The village school
1. Great Britain. Villages. Schools
1800–1987
I. Title
371'00941

ISBN 0–7090–3714–7

Photoset in Sabon by
Derek Doyle & Associates, Mold, Clwyd.
Printed in Great Britain by
St Edmundsbury Press Ltd, Bury St Edmunds, Suffolk.
Bound by WBC Bookbinders Limited.

For Matthew, Andrew and Gemma
my dear godchildren –
children of my former pupils –
children themselves of
the village school

Contents

Illustrations

PICTURE CREDITS

The author wishes to thank the following for permission to reproduce photographic material. Mrs J.E. Atkinson: 2. L. John Mayes: 3–4. Miss Phyllis Sayell: 5. Edward Payne: 9. C. Wedgbury: 10. Mrs Rita Gleghorn: 12, 32. Alan H. Dudeney: 14. Wookey Hole Caves: 15. Peter G. Holland: 18. R.J. Dempster: 21. Bryan Green: 26. Douglas Robinson: 28, 59. George Swinford: 33–5. David M. Richardson: 37. Roger Clark: 38. J.A. Morgan: 39. Christopher Wood: 40. G.L. Moore: 41. Gwynedd Archives Service: 46. Welsh Folk Museum: 47. Ministry of Education and Science: 48. *Derby Evening Telegraph*: 50. Mrs Irene Hickling: 53. E. Gutsell: 55. Reuben Sims: 56. A.F. Langham: 62–3. Alexander Gibson (courtesy of Frank Gibson): 64. Frank Gibson: 65. All other photographs by the author.

Acknowledgements

I am extremely grateful to all the Headteachers of the schools mentioned in this book for their co-operation and interest. My thanks also to numerous Education Officers, Archivists and Librarians of various County Councils. In particular I acknowledge the help of the following who gave freely of their time and allowed me access to their records.

Mrs Anne Bamford, Bushdown School, Selborne
Mrs Pamela Barnard and Patrick Barney, Abinger Hammer School Trust, Stelling Minnis
George B. Beaumont, Laughton-en-le-Morthen
Beechams Foods, *re* Horlicks
L.J. Beldham, Cuckney
G.H. Bunting, Castle Cary Preservation Society
S.H.D. Cassidy, Harenc School, Foots Cray
M.I. Constable, Defence Land Agency
Mrs P.M. Cottle, Coates School
W.E. Draycott, Bedfordshire
Alan Dudeney, St Richards with St Andrews School
Richard Edwards, Llanfair
Jeremy Fennell, Sen. Rural Administrative Officer NCVO
Forestry Commission
Mrs Rita Gleghorn, Swarland
Alison and Lesley Gooch, A-level Studies
Mrs E.I. Goodacre, Nottinghamshire
Ruth Gordon, Derbyshire County Library
Bryan Green, Dame Anna Child's School
D.C. Green, Department of the Environment
Miss Sylvia Greenwood, Ham, Richmond-on-Thames
Mrs Alice Mary Hadfield. *re* Chartists
Mrs Roma Hames, Godshill School
H.A. Hanley, County Archivist, Bucks.
Mrs Margaret Hartmann, Daglingworth School
P.J. Hayward, Lady Seaward's School
A. Heslop, Ardeley School
Mrs Irene Hickling, Little Melton
Peter Holland, Cheriton Fitzpaine
D.M. Holland, Berkhamsted Schools
Gordon Hutchings, BBC Producer
The Revd. W. Jacobson, Vicar of Clyst St George
M. Jones, East Ilsley

A.F. Langham, *re* Lundy
A.C. Lavender, Wookey Hole
Josaff Lewis, Borthygest
John E. Little, Curator, Tom Brown's School Museum
H. Lloyd, Hanmer
L. John Mayes, *re* Lace Schools
Ministry of Defence
G.L. Moore, Aston Fence J. and I. School
Allan G. Nash, Litton School
Mrs Mary Paget, Charlton Kings Local History Society
Sid Pender, Royal Society of Cornwall
Dr O.G. Pickard, Dunwich Museum
Miss Pat Pinnell, Sapperton School
R.H. Pratt, Berkswell
Alwyn Rea, County Personnel Officer, Gloucester
Alun Roberts, *re* Ysgol Borthygest
C.D. Robertson, Woodchurch School
Douglas Robinson, Sledmere
Mrs J.E. Robinson, Librarian, Keble College, Oxford University
Tony Saunders, Senior Education Officer, Gloucestershire County Council
Mrs I. Smith, Byrness Village School
Mrs Isobel Smith-Cresswell, Drayton Parslow
Mrs Molly Stiles, NASSS
George Swinford and George Swinford (Sen.), Filkins
Sir Tatton Sykes, Sledmere
Mrs Helen Terry, St Martins, Isles of Scilly
Mrs Joan Titcombe, Avebury
The Warden, Dudley Teachers Centre
Mrs Venice Watkins, *re* Gorsley Goff's School
Dr Eurwyn Wiliam, Keeper, Welsh Folk Museum
Stanley Witts, *re* Gorsley Goff's School
Christopher Wood, Sir John Moore School
Professor E.C. Wragg, Exeter University
Stanley G. Yardley, Wordsley
Mrs Evelyn Young, Gorsley

Introduction

School is an emotive word; the village school is evocative.

Few social reforms have generated as much heat and excitement as education has, does and will since the urgency to redress the imbalance between an élite ecclesiastical intellect and mass ignorance and inadequacy of an expanding population in the industrial nineteenth century gave the thrust to make school a national concern and responsibility. Now, just over a century later, education is again in a revolutionary state as the Baker Act is fighting its way through Parliament – potentially of equal historic significance as the great Forster Act of 1870.

Historically significant is that the core of the controversial national curriculum is the Three R's – the very heart of the old school time-table so scholastic history appears to be going full circle. But this is not an educational treatise, it is a look at the whole panorama of the education structure and development condensed into the

Fourteen sets of twins in one school brought the television cameras to Farmor's School and set up a national record

microcosm of a village; nowhere is the period and environment more vividly interwoven, and nothing more powerful in its local interpretation than the village school.

The definition of a village itself becomes more tenuous as time goes on: historical records refer to what are obvious villages as townships, the word village appears a fairly recent 'elevation', and many small places which can lay claim to ancient charters conferring on them the status of a market town cling tenaciously to that of a village – so it is not unusual to find a town hall in a village street! Classifications by the Department of Education and Science are relatively arbitrary, with 'rural' encompassing small towns and seaside resorts. A search through the database threw up only forty-six schools in England and Wales having 'Village' in its name – of which fourteen were colleges and one school in Inner London!

How do you define a village was the question most asked of me during my research for this book, and that in itself warranted a further exploration because the school more than any other institution adopts the character of its community. After much research and deliberation, I have taken the simple advice of a well-travelled publishing friend, 'a place is a village if the inhabitants think it is, and more specifically, a village ought to have a focal point that is not municipal'.

The school as the focal point of the village is therefore the subject of this study of some of the hundreds of village schools throughout the kingdom; few lay claim to fame through their teachers, old boys or old girls; even their very founding may at first glance seem ordinary – a median step from erratic inadequacy, founded on charity and fostered by faith and hope to lawful coercion, motivated by political pressure from the religious bodies who had neither power or resources to impose national legislation. Few, if any, battles have been fought on their playing fields. Few, if any, started off with a playing field; physical education did not feature in the early curriculum. And country children had enough fields to cross on their long walk to school.

The village school has been a vital and vibrant weft woven across the warp of village life for, at least, the last century; its story is the very fabric of our social history. Quaint and curious are some of the records, but never dull for within the pages of the Log Books and between the lines of the Reports are the very stuff of which village schools are made. Computers have replaced the slate and videos the blackboard in the classrooms; canned drinks, crisps and chips the bread and lard and cold water or just plain hunger of dinner-times; smart uniforms the cut-down hand-me-downs; buses the long walks on rough roads in ill-fitting boots and educational journeys abroad the Treat on the Vicarage lawn, but here, still, is the village school of

Wordsworth and Hardy, of Miss Read and Laurie Lee.

Here, is the village school where the local weather eclipsed the national news; here is the Headmistress who rang the School bell for a whole hour at the declaration of peace because her son was at the Front; here are the struggles for authority between the parson and master, and master and pupil. Here are the human stories. This is only right and proper for education is of people and school is a story of continuity – and schoolchildren live forever. And we thank God for that.

1 *The Early Years*

The Coming of Education

Education makes a people easy to lead,
  but difficult to drive,
  easy to govern,
but impossible to enslave.
Henry, Baron Brougham

The history of education in Britain begins with the coming of Christianity. The first Church School was founded in the sixth century, and teaching of sufficient Latin grammar and reading to get the brethren through the masses and responses was in the hands of the monasteries. From the collegiate churches and cathedrals developed the early grammar and song schools. The historical significance of education being a matter of ecclesiastical law was quoted in the House of Lords on an Education Bill in 1839, citing as the example the grammar school masters of Gloucester bringing a writ of trespass in 1410 against another master who had set up a school in the same town. Monastic education continued through the Middle Ages.

The Reformation raised the standard of education in the few schools that survived the sweeping changes; priests were replaced by men of letters in the chantry and charity schools, and early endowments contained specific clauses as to the academic and moral qualifications of the master. Elizabethan clergy, drawn from a more scholarly background, became respected key figures in the community and some pursued the teaching aspects of their pastoral duties, setting up reading groups in the church porch or gallery. Social changes worked in opposing directions at the Civil War and Commonwealth period: on the one hand education was seen as a radical reform to free men's minds; on the other, it was feared that the ability to read seditious publications was the most deadly weapon against authority.

Against a long history of intermittent attempts to educate the poor people were the crusading individuals. And from the seeds they

Lovington National School, Somerset. Founded in 1716 on rent from pasture land to school the poor village children 'for ever'

scattered, often on stony ground, so many of our village schools developed.

CHARITY AND DAME SCHOOLS

Nay, you cannot ordinarily find a servant in Scotland but he can read or write.

Daniel Defoe

As early as 1700 the majority of Scottish villages had their own, local rate-supported schools. But south of the border things were very different.

It is estimated that in 1818 only twenty-five per cent of the children of England received any education at all, and half the adult population 'made their mark' on the marriage registers by 'signing' with a cross, being totally incapable of writing their own name. Educationally backward, England had only a dual system to offer a few children some form of learning: the private schools – usually 'dame schools' run by purportedly educated ladies who charged a small fee for very elementary lessons, and the charity schools – financed by the interest rates on old endowments, donations and 'school pence'.

Dame Schools usually attracted derogatory remarks from contemporary educationalists. Caleb Parfectt, while a Curate at Uffington in Berkshire wrote to SPCK in 1712 that 'he shall to the utmost of his Power chearfully promote their designs ... that the Town is overrun with Quakers, and a Quaker woman keeps a school there, where they are brought up in such Ignorance that he could never find three of her schollars (tho' of competent age) able to repeat ye Lord's Prayer and ye Creed).' Whether the criticism was entirely justified on total incompetence or on sectarian grounds is open to conjecture.

However, the early Dame Schools tended to be of a more respectable and gentle class than the majority of those set up by 'child-minders' exploiting the situation of mothers being forced to go out to work in the 1830s and 40s. Teaching was often secondary to the teacher's main occupation which ranged from laundrymaid to toll-keeper. In the absence of any records having been kept, or surviving, there can be no judgement on, if there were any, curriculum or regulations. The only glimpses into these schools behind the lace curtains are those afforded by reading between the lines of the established schools' Log Books, where remarks followed the lines that children admitted from the local Dame School 'did not know their letters', and handed down stories.

Local tradition claims that the nicknames of Battle Murder and

Sudden Death, dubbed on the Misses Bradley who ran the Dame School in Valley House after the Housmans left, were given them by Edward and Sarah Jane's children. A. E. Housman had walked from Valley House in Fockbury to the sixteenth-century school at Bromsgrove for his own education.

At Selborne, Mary Neale of Huckers Lane was described as a dame school mistress in 1851, at the age of eighty-six. As one old dame said, 'Tis not much they pays me and it aint much I learns 'em'.

In 1776 on the Isle of Ely, an enterprising villager was offering (according to the inscription over the door of his house):

> Shaving done at a peny each. Hare oiled and powdered into the bargain. Also reding, Riting and Spelin taught according to the rules of Grammer, and caer takin of there Morels at 6d a week.

Promoting that good design of erecting catechetical schools had started in 1698 with the founding of SPCK – the Society for the Promotion of Christian Knowledge. The Society was the first central authority for elementary education through 'inclining the hearts of generous and well-disposed persons to contribute towards the erecting of schools' to remedy the decay of religion due to 'the barbarous ignorance observable among the common people'. Hornbooks, primers, writing books, Testaments and *The Whole Duty of Man* – a book of moral precepts – were supplied to most schools, together with bread and clothing for the needy.

Charity schools sprang up all over the country in the eighteenth century. But, as the need to earn became greater than the need to learn, endowments diminished in value or subscribers slipped in their support – so vital to the meagre budget of the village school, the charity school movement lost momentum in the economic and social changes of the industrial and agrarian revolutions at the latter end of the century.

The Church revived its ancient role as a seat of learning – but unlike the medieval grammar schools, the new age of increasing technology demanded more than a fair scribe's hand and a knowledge of the scriptures. Compromising between basic elementary education and upholding its religious principles, the Sunday School movement linked the past with the future, maintained the ethos of the early charity schools, and contributed to the nation's educational resources before the State reluctantly assumed a degree of responsibility.

SUNDAY SCHOOLS

Robert Raikes has been acclaimed as the father of the Sunday School movement, but Sunday teaching had been conducted in his native

Gloucestershire villages for at least half a century before Raikes opened his first school in 1780. A weaver of Painswick was gathering the children from the Sheepscombe Valley into his cottage for Sunday lessons in 1720, and the beautiful Catherine Boevey of Flaxley Abbey who died in 1726 – the 'Perverse Widow' who distracted Sir Roger de Coverley – is recorded on her memorial as 'clothing and feeding her indigent neighbours and teaching their children, some of whom every Sunday by turns she entertained at her house and examined them herself'.

What Robert Raikes did was to raise the lot of neglected children which he found to be 'ignorant, profane, filthy and ignorant in the extreme', observing through his experience as a prison reformer the relationship between ignorance and crime, by making local instances a universal institution.

Another Gloucestershire man, William Fox who rose from a poor ploughboy and bird-scarer to become Lord of the Manor of his home village of Clapton, high on the Cotswold Hills, spearheaded the Sunday School Society. Fox also started and supported a day school at Clapton about 1795.

Sunday Schools of both the established church and Non-conformists offered an educational life-line and were set up all over the country; 'school' varied from a group of children huddled on benches in a corner of the church or chapel to specially built schoolrooms attached to them. Teachers were paid one shilling a week for their services; the tradition of voluntary teaching of Sunday School only started when state education was established.

A time-table or Rules as it was described, for a Sunday School 'on Mr Raikes's plan' give an insight on a child's Sunday in 1815.

8.30 a.m.	Assembly, with clean hands and face and hair combed
8.45	Roll call
9.00	Morning hymn. Prayer. Collect, followed by Reading and Spelling
10.00	Catechism, all children to stand round room and repeat with a loud and distinct voice
10.25	Church, orderly and quietly to take their respective seats. Children who can read to take a Prayerbook. Dismissal
1.30 p.m.	Assembly. Reading and Spelling
2.30	Church. After service, return to schoolroom for evening hymn and dismissal

Its success was gauged by Raikes measuring the order and 'exercise of the benevolence which Christianity peculiarly recommends' in the Stroud valley mill villages. In 1786 crowds thronged in from the countryside to celebrate Painswick Feast, which, according to

Raikes, was an excuse for 'every species of clamour, riot and disorder', to be sobered by the impressive assembly of some 331 Sunday School children being inspected by the gentry outside the church. Of these, 230 could read, 80 were learning, with the rest 'in the alphabet'. A little boy of Thrupp had in one week 'though daily employed at the mill, committed to memory 400 verses of hymns'.

The Nonconformists welcomed the Sunday School movement as a means of providing elementary education under their own control, divorced from the doctrine of the established church. For the children whose religious following was rooted more in which schoolroom was warmer, which lessons the least exacting, or which sermons less tedious, there was the attraction of the Sunday School Treats. If one spread one's devotions fairly equally it was possible to enjoy the junketings of both church and chapel.

Raikes the Anglican and Fox the Baptist, working together for a unified system, spearheaded an educational movement from which the curriculum, organisation and even teaching methods sprang in later day schools, for Raikes had used a monitorial scheme by setting older children to help teach the younger, at least a decade before Bell or Lancaster gave their names to it.

School on Sundays left the weekdays free for the children to pursue their employment on the farm, in mills and factories and down the mines – in 1842, boys of six years of age were hauling baskets of coal underground in the Forest of Dean coal pits or in the blasting heat of the ironworks, earning vital pennies to help poverty-stricken households. Even so, there was opposition from employers, especially 'gentlemen farmers' and some landed gentry who regarded Sunday Schools as seditious centres for 'Jacobinism' and 'Methodism' and many objected on principle to the labouring poor being encouraged to read and write for fear they might no longer be content with their place in society.

SCHOOLS OF INDUSTRY AND RAGGED SCHOOLS

The early nineteenth century was a revolutionary period in the history of education, and the village became a community divided between charity and Dame Schools and Sunday Schools, of different denominations. A situation aggravated, rather than alleviated, by the introduction of schools of industry. Schools of industry were an attempt to counter the criticism levelled against the charity schools – which was that children of the poor were not taught the labouring skills for which they were destined to earn their living.

Hannah More summarized her plan of instruction for the Mendip schools, which received a great deal of publicity: 'They learn on weekdays such coarse work as may fit them for servants. I allow of no writing for the poor ...' The pupils were taught obedience, reading, knitting and spinning. Hannah More devoted her immense talents and energy to the service of education at a time of appalling indifference and robust opposition. Withdrawing from London's sparkling social circle where she counted Sir Joshua Reynolds, Burke, Goldsmith and Johnson among her friends, to the Somerset hamlet of Cowslip Green she resolved to educate the ignorant countryfolk both in morals and literacy. In the village of Cheddar she found but one Bible – and that was used as a stand for a flowerpot. Resolutely overcoming obstinacy and virulent persecution, Hannah More and her sisters set up schools in the Mendips for some sixteen hundred children. She turned her writing talent from drama and poetry to educational tracts: *Strictures on the Modern System of Female Education* was published in 1799, and won the rare honour of 'a public episcopal encomium'; followed by *Hints for the Education of a Princess*, which was adopted as a guide for Princess Charlotte's education – the subject of an audience with the Queen.

The School of Industry experiment set its stronger roots in the old market towns where there was a long tradition of industry. At Cirencester, a centre for the medieval wool trade, a Yellow School was set up in 'a strong house' in Gloucester Street where boys wove worsted stockings and girls learnt spinning; but 'the goods were much complained of' and the masters proved 'ignorant and indolent', and it closed in 1814 after a Chancery enquiry.

More enduring were those which trained girls for domestic service. A Mrs Williams founded The School of Industry in 1807 in a converted thatched barn down the road from her home village of Prestbury, in a lane off the London end of Cheltenham. It gained much local prestige and royal patronage from Queen Charlotte and Queen Victoria, who became its patron in 1843, by which time it was limited to orphan girls.

In country schools the scheme was often introduced within the set curriculum but even small places like the village of Adlestrop, immortalised by Edward Thomas, had a school of industry in 1803 where 16 children were taught to read and knit.

Better build schoolrooms for 'the boy',
Than cells and gibbets for 'the man'.

Eliza Cook, A Song for the Ragged Schools

The Ragged Schools movement aimed at preventing the poorest of the miserable poor from resorting to crime as a livelihood. Inducing attendance by offering the children a decent meal, they took the form of 'Industrial Schools' where, in addition to the three R's and scripture, the boys could learn such useful work as tailoring and shoemaking, and the girls laundrywork and sewing. Taken from the 'criminal and abandoned classes' the children would not have been encouraged to attend the National and British schools so did much to civilise the juvenile underworld before compulsory education. Lord Ashley, the factory reformer, became President of the Ragged Schools Union in the 1850s. A champion of its cause, his Lordship was not above begging money for the schools from MPs as they entered Parliament.

A School for 'ragged children' was started in the Latin School, which is now the Agricultural College, London University, by Lady Joanna Thornhill in the seventeenth century. Lady Joanna also founded the village school at Wye in Kent; the original room being in Wye College, once a Latin School.

Not only the land, but the local water supply is owned by the founding charity at Whitton in Powys. The village school was endowed from the rents of 150 acres by Dame Anna Child, and the school – founded in 1724 – is named after its benefactress.

LACE SCHOOLS

Nineteen long lines hang over my door,
The harder I work the shorter my score;
The more I do play, it sticks at a stay –
So come, little fingers, let's twink away.
There's twinkum and twankum, and five to your four;
Them as are done first, they may give o'er.

Old lace tell

Lace schools held a unique place in the history of education, if for no other reason than the grim reality behind the romantic nomenclature. Nimble little fingers 'twinking away' at their bobbin-spangled pillows conjure up a picture of old-world charm and tranquillity, but the schools were no more than cramped cottages, where groups of small children were gathered together under an eagle-eyed local dame to make fine bone lace as a cottage industry controlled by hard master merchants.

Lace-making centred mainly in Buckinghamshire and north Bedfordshire in the sixteenth century when the Flemings fled from Catholic persecution to Protestant England, bringing their craft skills with them. The Elizabethans and Stuarts used lace lavishly; demand and profitability dictated the rise of lace schools, which at their peak employed both boys and girls and greatly outnumbered any other type of school. There were 63 villages known to have lace schools in Buckinghamshire 1750-1850.

The earliest reference to training children at lace-making is in 1596, when the overseers' accounts for Eaton Socon showed that Goodwife Clarke was paid twopence a week for teaching each child. The few pennies that the children earned were vital in poverty-ridden

Widow Dobbin's Lace School at Stokenchurch, *c.* 1860. The old house, now demolished, stood opposite the church gate

households. The indifference to the ability of little folk at the time is revealed by the Buckinghamshire vicar, who rebuked the parishioners for applying for parish relief by thundering forth from the pulpit: 'any industrious child of 5 should be able to support itself'. At Mrs Dobbin's lace school at Stokenchurch toddlers as young as three years of age were accepted as pupils at a fee of 2d per week.

Overseers of the poor made good use of the lace industry either by paying for poor children to be taught lace-making or setting up their own schools, usually attached to the workhouse. Records of lace schools are scarce but extracts from the Minutes of the one at Emberton village, established in the 'Old School' at the relatively late date of 1822 give an insight of a school where the money earned from their lace-making paid for the pupils' lessons and board.

That Mrs Fry, Mrs Cropwell, Mrs Thomas Hale and Mrs Horry be requested to select 6 children as fit objects to be admitted into the day school.

That the Parents should be permitted to see their Children at the School once a week on such day and hour as the Committee shall hereafter determine. That the Children should have a holiday once a quarter to go home to see their Parents. But the privilege is not to be extended to the mother of Ann Caves who would only be allowed to see her child in the presence of the Master and Mistress of the School, and as the Committee may direct, and the child not to be permitted to visit her Mother in the Poor House.

The School closed in 1831 after two of the 'objects' had died.

A charity, by will of Sir William Borlase in 1628, financed the education of twenty-four poor boys to read, write and cast accounts and twenty 'poor women children' to knit, spin and make bone lace in the Marlow area. The charity, which extended to Little Marlow and Medmenham, was still operating in the 1830s when a schoolmistress was teaching twelve girls to read, make lace and do plain work free of fee and provided with 'a bonnet, frock, tippet sleeves and apron'.

Protection of the delicate work governed the conditions under which the children worked and, indirectly, created the foundation for the scanty formal education they received. Smoke from open fires would have dirtied the fine lace so heating was by means of the 'dicky' or 'chaddy' pot – an earthenware pot was filled with hot embers and placed under the lace-makers' skirts.

Breaks from the tedium of the work were essential, but the children were not allowed outside to play for fear of getting their hands dirty, for water drawn from the well was scarcely enough for the dame's household needs. It was during these breaks that reading and recitation, with a little writing were taught, and it is interesting that many a marriage register in 'laceland' shows the bridegroom's 'mark' as a cross whereas the bride, if a lacemaker, had signed her name in a bold hand.

The Evidence given to the Children's Employment Commission of 1867 refers specifically to lace schools in Bedfordshire at Wilhampstead, Elstow, Houghton Conquest and Cotton End. Trade was already declining through competition from cheaper, machine-made lace, but the lace-makers clung in desperation to their meagre livelihood, and the 'novel strike' of 1867 in the Buckinghamshire hamlet of Gawcott, where one-third of the female population were lace-makers, attracted the attention of *The Times* and Karl Marx.

It was from this period that the grim details of the lace schools emerge: tales handed down through families tell of young girls having to bend over their pillows to be caned across the shoulders, and little boys hung on to the ceiling beam by a cord under their arms, for failing to produce the expected length of lace in a day. One child recalled, 'when I was five, my mother took me to the lace school and gave the teacher a shilling. She learnt me for an hour, smacked my head six times, and rubbed my nose on the pin-heads'.

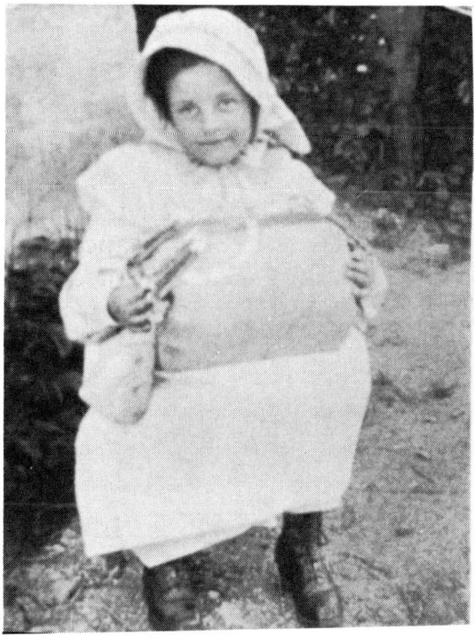

A little lace-schoolgirl

Lace-tells were chanted by the children between the reading and writing lessons to relieve the monotony, and were encouraged for their self-imposed discipline. Rewards were few and far between; a specially industrious child might earn an inscribed bobbin for his or her pillow commemorating a hanging or suicide – the 'treat' of taking the child to witness a hanging was the parent's prerogative.

In some lace schools the children were allowed a 'locking-out day' when they kept the teacher out of the room until the promise of a half-day holiday was extracted. The two main celebrations were Cattern's Day on 25 November to be followed by Tander's Day on 30 November.

Straw plait schools were established in the south-east Midlands and in the 'lace counties' about 1800, although straw hat making had provided some 14,000 people with a living since Stuart times. The plait schools were little more than 'sweat shops'. Social distinctions were drawn between the lace and plait girls particularly – the former looking down on the latter.

With the introduction of elementary education in 1870, many schools had to include lace-making or plaiting in their curriculum to stimulate attendance, but generally the parents resisted – ill affording to lose the extra earnings made by the children.

14 Feb. 1879 — Many of the girls absent this week – kept home to plait straw, there being a slight improvement in the plait trade.

Drayton Parslow, Bucks.

Church and State: The Beginnings of a National System

The ruling class was reluctant to interfere with the 'voluntary principle' – although many feared that education of the poor would enlighten them on their servile position, leading to dissatisfaction and even revolution. But a rising population in a society which was moving into an industrial and commercial age needed educated workers. After a period of futile wrangling and indecision, a government grant of £20,000 was made in 1833 to aid private subscription for the erection of schools for the education of the children of the 'Poorer Classes' – the sum was equally divided between the two denominational societies. The British System for the Education of the Labouring and Manufacturing Classes of Society of Every Religious Persuasion was reduced to a more pronounceable British and Foreign Schools Society in 1814, and more locally to just plain British. A mere two words shorter was The National Society for the Education of the Poor in the Principles of the Established Church established in 1811. This, as its name implies, originated strictly for Anglican children, but broadened its brief as it shortened its name to the National Society. Many villages can trace both British and National schools in their history.

'Consideration of all matters affecting the education of the people' was of direct concern of Queen Victoria. It was at her instigation that

Sombre and serious at Drayton Parslow, *c.* 1907

a Privy Council Committee was set up in 1839 to superintend the application of any sums of money voted by Parliament for this purpose, under the secretaryship of Dr Kay Shuttleworth – a key figure in educational progress. One of the important steps resulting from the brief was that, from 1840, bodies not associated with either the National Society or the British Society were eligible for grants towards the building or extension of a school. This released schools from specific religious authority, although there was the stipulation that grants were conditional on there being daily scripture readings and that such schools should be open to inspection by government inspectors.

Many schools however did become enfranchised at a later date to be recognised as Church of England Schools.

The whole business of education was the sole concern of the individual community. Whether a school was provided at all and how it was maintained depended on the interest and financial support of local people. In 1858 a Royal Commission on Education reviewed the position, concluded from their survey that only one in eight of the total child population attended a day school, and, recognising the urgent need for universal elementary education, produced practical recommendations. Putting these into practice was impeded by innate conservatism of those who could afford to subsidise the education of those who could not, and the reluctance of the government to get embroiled in the opposing interests of the Established Church and the Nonconformists.

EDUCATION ACTS

Gladstone's Bill of 1870, under the guidance of W. E. Forster, wrought important changes in education. It was a historical step made by the Government to take a positive interest in educating its citizens and in the building of schools after a reluctance to become involved in what other modern countries saw as a vital national concern.

The State Grant to existing schools was doubled, and set up publicly controlled Board Schools, to be paid for out of local rates and governed by elected School Boards.

The Board Schools bridged the gaps between the church and charity schools. The Boards, elected by ratepayers, were established to make up deficiencies in educational cover. Often it was not until the Education Department issued a final order that the Board realised their first duty – that of determining the amount of school accommodation to be provided for the district. The country was divided into school districts that corresponded with the parishes and boroughs.

The two voluntary societies, National and British, were pressed to improve their provision for education before the end of 1870 and failing a satisfactory outcome gave the ratepayers the right to elect a School Board that could use money from the rates with help from the Government.

As in the case of Besthorpe in Nottinghamshire, there was already a National School under the charge of an uncertificated teacher, and the School Board requested transfer to the Board; sometimes the existing premises were suitable, more often they were not and new schools were built – the ratepayers picking up the cost.

Church teaching was to be continued in the voluntary schools, but in Board Schools the use of the Catechism or 'formulary distinctions of any denomination' was prohibited. It was not easy to legislate a doctrine approved by both the established Church and the Nonconformists. The Education Act offered a compromise, but not a policy, on how education should be provided and by its liberality opened a chasm of controversy. The supporters of the non-denominational Board Schools wanted education freed of religious dogma, while those who supported the National Schools wanted to preserve religious instruction, so in villages up and down the country the Church was still fighting for control of the schools even when local opinion was against it.

The evangelical teaching of John Wesley was firmly rooted in many, particularly industrially depressed, areas and the Dissenters strongly resisted the authoritarian claims of Established Church – the Methodists particularly became actively engaged in setting up their own schools where there was no sectarian teaching, although they expected the pupils to attend Sunday School.

It was universally acknowledged that religious teaching should be given in all schools, but the deep rift was at denominational level. The 'Cowper Temple amendment' offered the compromise by adding the Conscience Clause to the new Education Act of 1870 so that all schools were compatible on religious education. This was achieved by giving religious instruction at time-tabled periods, with the option to parents to withdraw their children from those lessons 'on grounds of conscience'.

It was the Education Act of 1902 which forged a truce between Anglicans and Dissenters. Parity of treatment was further tempered by increased allowances for educational equipment – at last the schools were released from the yoke of earning a grant and servility to the Vicar. The shift of power emboldened many a master.

Received a strong complaint from a parent that the Vicar had stopped children on their way from school and questioned them on school matters. I wrote to the Rev pointing out to him that I should be pleased to answer any questions he wishes to put upon School matters.

Uffington, Berks, 1906

In the strong chapel country of Wales the principles of school boards were generally welcomed as a means of diminishing the influence of the Church of England. However, as in England, the introduction of compulsory elementary education and how it should be organised became a political issue from county to county and parish to parish. The opposition of the Anglicans to a school board in the Nonconformist parish of Ynyscynhaearn – where the first British School in North Wales was established in 1816 – forced an election to gauge the opinion of the ratepayers in 1871. The result was a surprising defeat and the schools had to support themselves until bankruptcy forced one at Porthmadog to close in 1877.

The advantages of coming under the aegis of a school board were realised; a second election voted for a board and this was established.

Many village schools for one reason or another were never church schools. Abinger Hammer's school was built by the agnostic T.H. Farrer, Liberal Lord of the Manor and his equally determined son, Thomas Cecil, and remained a voluntary school that was not a church school for thirty-one years.

I told him that we had no distinctive religious teaching in our schools there really was no object in not handing them over to the

The early seventeenth-century school at Tom Brown's village in the Vale of thc White Horse

County Council.

Miss Forster, Abinger Hammer, 18 June 1905

Sheriff Hutton's new school replaced two old buildings; one a Methodist foundation, the other a Church of England foundation – divided by the main road and other factors. The schism has been further bridged by the diplomacy of the Head holding Education Day services in both churches.

The Education Act of 1902, generally referred to as the Balfour Act, tied together the threads of the diverse systems which had run chaotically through the Voluntary and Board Schools. Anomalies of funding and administration, revealed through the Bryce Commission of 1896, were ironed out by the co-ordination of policies with control centred on the newly formed Local Education Authorities.

Education for every child was now assured, financed by government grants to the authority, and a levied education rate on each county. Relieved of the burden of making ends meet, schools were now obliged to conform with its authority's regulations, with an agreed time-table.

Integration replaced independence. Divisional officers and auditors from 'the County' checked the registers which the school correspondent – usually the vicar from the vicarage next door – once did. Advisers, not the Lady of the Manor, inspected the needlework and 'listened to the singing'. The Education Authority, not the Vicar or influential landowner, set the dates of the school holidays regardless of whether or not there was 'much corn abroad'.

The Education Act of 1918, largely the work of H. A. L. Fisher, fixed the school-leaving age at fourteen and restricted the employment of schoolchildren to little more than delivering newspapers. The Second World War brought into focus more shortcomings of the educational system. The recommendation of the Hadow Report of 1926, which criticised the 'all-age schools' where children spent their entire school life in the same building, was the main objective of the 'free secondary education for all' of the 1944 Act, piloted through Parliament by R. A. Butler. The word 'elementary', with its connotations of inferiority, disappeared and children were transferred at the age of 11 to secondary or grammar schools.

By virtue of its size, the village school became a Primary or Infant school, and it is at this village school, the historic heart of its community, that we look now.

FUNDING AND SCHOOL PENCE

Schools were meant to be financially self-supporting. The income derived from four main sources: endowments – which were fixed;

Laughton-en-le-Morthen, Yorks. The oldest part of the school – nearest the road – dates back to the early seventeenth century

local subscriptions – which were never very generous; government grant – which was variable and dependant upon many factors beyond the Headteacher's control; school pence – which, again, was a fluctuating sum, difficult to impose and an onerous duty of the Head to collect. From the combined income came the teacher's salaries, educational books and equipment, maintenance of the buildings, heating, lighting and cleaning. The problems in providing a local education service as a viable proposition were national and legion.

Illustrative of the policy pursued in individual communities is gleaned from a letter written by the Revd T. Rigby from Laughton Vicarage, Rotherham in January 1899 to Col. John St Leger, stating that 'unless the amount of the voluntary rate is paid in lieu of the present subscription, the schools will be nearly £40 in debt. If you, as the largest Landowner, agree to pay the annual amount of the proposed rate I shall immediately apply to all the other property owners who have not hitherto agreed to pay the Voluntary Rate'.

When school pence was introduced many parents who were opposed already to the compulsory education which prevented their children earning wages, considered this deprivation an affront – and, in far too many cases, an impossibility.

The weekly fees varied from county to county, Board to Board and school to school, but nowhere was it to be more than 9d a week.

Lately arrears in weekly payments have been difficult to recover. Some parents plead inability owing to want of employment on the father's part, but in others it is neglect and habit of indifference.

All Saints, Laughton-en-le-Morthen, W. Yorks., 1878

The Rev Mr Cooper proposed to arrange the fees so that the labourers pay 2d for the first child and 1d for others, other people to pay 3d for each child. (This system was abandoned 4 months later.)

Abinger Hammer Minute Book, 7 July 1880

The colliers are still on strike and in consequence many boys are in arrears with their fees.

Netherton, Worcs., 1884

School pence finally ceased in 1891.

PAYMENT BY RESULTS

'We must educate our masters'.

Robert Lowe, (later first Viscount Sherbrook) is generally remembered more for the iniquitous Payment by Results system, which he introduced as part of the Revised Code than his succinct reference to the newly enfranchised working classes during his Parliamentary speech on the Reform Bill of 1867.

The Payment of Results, introduced in 1861 was the spectre, manifested as the Annual Inspection, which haunted Headteachers (in modified form) until 1895 – outliving its author by four years. Payment of the grant was based on the conditions laid down in the Code of 1871 and subsequent revisions, and was totally dependant on attendance, attainment and the condition of the premises. Fulfilling all three criteria was beyond the power of the headteachers and Log Books up and down the country paint a picture of despondency and desperation.

Another rule of the Code was that personal expressions and opinions were prohibited: the Log Books, along with the pupils' reading, writing and singing; the staff conduct, and how much the windows opened or the chimney smoked or the 'offices' smelt, were all open to inspection, criticism and monetary evaluation.

To counter the imbalance of 'attendance' against 'times open', long-suffering Heads closed the registers, took the coals off the fire, and declared a holiday every time a Band of Hope, circus, farm sale (which often went on for days) or bun-fight drew the children away from the school door like the Pied Piper. Every attendance was of the utmost importance and errors in registration warranted an explanation in the Log Book.

16 Sept. 1895 One child in Standard I omitted to answer her name when the roll was called. Teacher was cautioned as to more watchfulness.

Farmor's, Fairford, Glos.

Achieving anything like a successful standard in the realms of attendance, attainment and 'efficiency of the premises' was further impeded by the unfair reliance of one upon the other – for in order to be eligible for the test of attainment the pupil had to have made a minimum number of attendances.

As well as the endemic seasonal causes for poor attendance, the village school was, and still is, the heart of the community – extending its role as village hall, parish polling station and emergency centre where there are no alternative premises of comparable size. No doubt due in part to the corporate possession fostered by the ratepayers supporting the school, local functions often took precedence over education and many a school had to close for an afternoon 'to oblige the Cricket Club who are preparing the schoolroom for their annual concert'.

ATTENDANCE

The causes for absenteeism in the early days were legion; every conceivable excuse kept the children from the classroom with its monotonous routine of uninspiring lessons, few of which equipped them for their destiny. In country areas it was the farming cycle, on the coastline it was the sea; and throughout the kingdom every local event and just anything out of the ordinary that would be cause for comment in quiet country places and isolated villages.

Absences caused by haymaking, turnip-singling, carrot-weeding, pea-pulling, potato-picking ... George Bennett was illegally employed all day by Mr Pigott, one of the members of the School Board ... The attendance this week is most miserable the average scarcely reaching 29 ... many children being employed in the fields.

Besthorpe, Notts., 1883

At one time a farmer had to pay more to a labourer with a big family, so a man's wealth was invariably counted by the number of his sons; often there was rivalry between employers for cheaper child labour.

8 April. 1899 Mr Coe stated that Ernest Bone had worked for him before school hours; that Mr Harrison had informed the parents that this was improper; that Ernest Bone then ceased to work for Mr Coe, but had since been employed by Mr Harrison.

Abinger Hammer Minute Book

19 Sept. 1884	Most of the children gone to see the circus at Porthmadog.
8 June 1913	Holiday because of the golf tournament at Morfa Bychan, some of the senior boys were caddies.

Ysgol Morfa Bychan, Gwynedd

Successive headteachers (usually female) complained in the log books of poor attendance at Widecombe through sheep-shearing, inability to pay school fees, chapel anniversary, wall building, potato-tilling, goose-plucking, fits and bad feet – and the famous Widecombe Fair.

Attendance in the early days was erratic to say the least; difficult to impose and almost totally reliant on what was going on in the village. Each season brought its restrictions and seductions. Rough roads in country districts became an impassable morass in winter's storm and hay meadows called for help at summer harvest; often it was the school managers themselves who gave permission for the children to be absent from school to swell the labour force in the fields, or beating for the squire's shoot, carrying the fishermen's baskets or helping at the hunt. Individual illnesses became serious epidemics and swept through families, classes and the whole village, fostered by overcrowding, suspect personal hygiene, poor sanitation, inadequate heating and ventilation and little or no medical care, forcing the school to close – occasionally with tragic loss of young life.

Ellen Hughes, a young girl, died during an epidemic in the village.
During the Christmas holiday the headmaster's son died of the epidemic.

Ysgol Borthygest, Gwynedd, 1893

The time for school holidays has always varied from county to county – even today – but at the turn of the century the summer holiday dates were governed by the regional seasonal harvest. September was the time for the great exodus from the Black Country, when whole families packed their meagre wardrobe into the 'hoppen box' and transported by train from their closely packed terrace houses which edged the streets backed by the nail and chain shops – as the garden sheds were called – exchanging the blow and batter of the bellows and anvil for the fresh air and friendly banter of the Hereford hopfields.

Catchment areas were practically ignored – the choice of school was often determined by factors quite unrelated to proximity or academic standing. Of the three Cradley schools in the Black Country, Netherend was particularly well attended by children from Quarry Bank when the school-leaving age was thirteen in Worcestershire, and fourteen in Staffordshire.

Mundella's Act of 1880 made obligatory the issue of local regulations to enforce the attendance at school of every child up to a leaving age of thirteen on attendance alone. But, even so, the effects on rural schools were usually minimal and the power of the School Boards ineffective.

Tregaron, set in the wild mountains of the Welsh sheeplands, was a central spot from which drovers started their long climb eastwards to the English markets beyond the spectacular Wye Valley. The hiring fair on New Year's Day always attracted the schoolchildren. Attendance was governed by the rural calendar of haymaking and peat harvest and every local happening.

1 Jan. 1876	Holiday for the children to collect calening.
27 Apr.	Fine weather, children harrowing.
10 June	No school – eisteddfod at Talsarn.

Gartheli, Tregaron, Dyfed

An Act to regulate the employment of children in agriculture was enforced in 1875 whereby:

no employer, or his agent, may employ any child under 8 in agricultural labour, unless he be its parent or guardian, and then only on land in his own occupation –

if the child be over 8 and under 10, he must have completed 250 school attendances (that is, 25 weeks at least) within the 12 months immediately preceding the issue of the certificate –

if he be over 10 and under 12, he must have completed 150 school attendances (that is, 15 weeks at least,) within the same period. (No children, whether boys or girls, can be exempted from these rules but those who have passed the 4th Standard) –

no child under the age of 10 years shall be employed in any agricultural gang.

Morning school and afternoon school each count as one attendance. The school must be a school recognised by Government as efficient, if there be one within 2 miles of the parent's home.

The Magistrates had the power to 'entirely suspend the Act during a few weeks in the busy seasons of the year.' The Act was not strictly adhered to, despite there being penalties of £5 against employers.

4 July 1884	Parents in this district do not seem to care for Education. As soon as a boy has passed 4th Standard, he leaves and goes to work. A sharp boy would be of course considerably under 13, so that the human part of the 'Agricultural Act' is a dead letter.

Farmor's, Fairford, Glos.

Inducement both moral and material was offered to tempt children to attend school regularly. Medallions inscribed Never Absent, Never Late were the most common rewards.

In 1880, the Headmaster of Borthygest School was offering a penny to every child that had not missed a day's schooling during the previous quarter, and those who had missed only one day were rewarded by a halfpenny. In 1902 R. Hughes received a gold medal for unbroken attendance of eight-and-a-half years – which must have been a record for such absence-riddled times.

Children who constantly attended Lovington School received gifts of warm clothes.

At Hemington, the School Board presented a book to each child who had made over 400 attendances in 1893. Books, usually bibles, were also the rewards for perfect attendance in the Black Country, with a silver watch for those lucky enough to escape illness and the need to 'skip school' to earn an extra penny to help the family income, in a total of five years.

Broughton-cum-Filkins, Oxon.: Grant for 1868 for 16 months ending 30 April

Average Attendance	72	
Deduct – not fulfilling Art 4	1	
Number for payment at	4s	71
Qualified for Examination	51	
Presented for Examination	46	
Passes in Standards I-III	96	
Passes in Standards IV-VI	16	
Passes in Reading	37	
Passes in Writing	40	
Passes in Arithmetic	35	
Number for payment at 2s 6d		112
Infants under 6 years of age	16 at 6s 6d.	

Day School: Gross Total of Claim = £45 15s 7d

Evening School

Average Attendance:	Females 10 at 2s 6d
Passes in Reading:	Males 11, Females 9
Passes in Writing:	Male 9, Females 8
Passes in Arithmetic:	Males 10, Females 9
	Total: 56 at 1s 8d

Evening School (1 Year) Gross Total of Claim = £5 18s 4d

MONITORS AND PUPIL TEACHERS

The National Society, founded in 1811, became the main educational agency of the Church of England. It adopted the mass instruction by child monitors known as the Madras System, invented by Dr Andrew Bell. The monitorial system, of setting the older children to teach the younger what they themselves had learnt, had been used by Robert Raikes with success in the Sunday School movement at least a decade before Bell or Lancaster claimed credit for its innovation.

An enthusiastic visitor to a Gloucestershire school exulted that the 'steady vigilance and assiduity marked the operations of the School, masters, monitors and boys being alertly engaged', to such a degree that 'on my return the following impromptu oozed out –

'As to Hope's gladd'ning eye, the Spring's bright face
Does Summer's flowers and Autumn's fruits reveal
So, in this teeming school array, we trace
Rich mental Harvests for the Public weal'.

The reality of the monitorial system was not such a poetic evocation. Monitors were often burdened at a very early age of about ten or eleven with responsibilities beyond the giving out of slates or books, preparing pens, making up the ink, ruling lines in the copy books and general factotum, extending to keeping order, elementary teaching and rounding up truants.

16 May 1872 — I wish the monitor [Robert Johnson employed at one shilling a week] had more spirit for teaching. He lets the children almost go to sleep and does the same thing himself.

Viney Hill National School, Glos.

Pupil teachers were considered an important part of the teaching strength in schools, and were mentioned in Log Books as early as 1863. An indenture dated 1881 specified that the pupil teacher should serve under a certificated teacher during the usual school hours up to thirty hours per week. The Head teacher was to instruct the pupil teacher for at least an hour each day 'while the school is not being held' – this followed an earlier circular to HM Inspectors to oppose the appointment of sickly and precocious children and to see that they were not overworked.

21 Sept. 1894 — Pupil Teachers come at 7 a.m. and after having prepared lessons they do Arithmetic till 8 when they go to breakfast and get back at 10 minutes to 9. Euclid and Poetry are usually said in the dinner hour.

Farmor's, Fairford, Glos.

In 1928 the Board of Education made a rule that pupil teachers received practical instruction in certain subjects. The pupil teacher apprenticeship was often six years or more, with an examination each year set by the visiting Inspector. On passing the examination a small stipend was paid to the pupil teacher and the instructor (normally the head teacher) received a supplement to his or her salary. On completion of his articles the pupil teacher sat for the Queen's Scholarship and was granted, if successful, a government certificate conferring qualified teacher status in different classes. Up-grading of the class could be achieved if HM Inspector gave a favourable report at the annual inspection of the school.

Extract from a letter regarding appointment of a scholar as Pupil Teacher.

Education Department, Privy Council Office
Downing Street London S W

24th June 1868

Broughton-cum-Filkins School

Revd Sir

I have the honour to inform you that ... The Committee of Council on Education agrees to the engagement of the following Scholar, viz –

Mary Jane Titchener (3rd Year)

as a Pupil Teacher ... from the first day of *May 1868*.

The enclosed Memorandum of Agreement should not be completed and signed until the several parties interested have thoroughly comprehended its terms; and each of them ought to procure a copy of the Code to which it refers. The price of this Code is 3d ... It should be described in the order of The Revised Code of Minutes and Regulations of the Committee of Council on Education.

If for any reason the engagement intended to be made in the accompanying stamped form is *not* entered into, the form should be returned to this office, in order that the cost of the stamp may be recovered. If it appears, from the next Report of the Inspector, that the stamped form, although retained, has not been used, the price of the stamp, 2s 6d, will be deducted from the Grant ...

My Lords further desire to bring under your consideration the importance of taking care that the Principal Teacher, and each Pupil Teacher, be furnished with a good Text Book ... At the close of each year, the Pupil Teachers are required to present certificates of good conduct from the Managers of the School, and of punctuality, diligence, obedience, and attention to their duties from the Schoolmaster or mistress ...

Summary of the Inspector's Report on the School
The condition of the School is very much improved, and reflects great credit upon the industry and skill of the Master and Mistress.

My Lords have sanctioned the engagement of Mary Jane Titchener at the beginning of the third year, on the understanding that the provisions of Article 81 (c) will be strictly observed in regard to her special instruction.

2 *Foundations*

ENDOWMENTS AND THE EARLY FOUNDERS

Our village was blessed amongst other things with a well-endowed school. The building stood by itself, apart from the master's house, on an angle of ground where three roads met; an old grey stone building with a steep roof and mullioned windows.

Tom Brown's Schooldays

Thomas Hughes was the first author to cast the school itself in the major role, as compared with the institutions portrayed by Brontë and Dickens, and the school was, of course, the now legendary Rugby – but before Hughes sent his fictional hero off to that great citadel he has him peeping in at the tiny village school, distracting the boys and incensing the master. The old school at Uffington was certainly 'well-endowed' by Thomas Saunders of Woolstone, and extracts from his will give specific rules about the school which was founded in 1617. Endowed with twenty acres of land, the rent was 'towarde the maynetenance and relieffe of the said Scholemaster for the teacheinge of twelve poore Schollars'. A Diocesan enquiry of 1686 confirms: 'In Uffington, in the County of Berks, There is a Schoole to breed up young Children, and the Governess of the Sayd Schoole is Mrs Ann Saunders of Woolston in the parish of the sayd Uffington, Widow.' Governess in this context meant Patroness. One of the clauses of the decree excluded girls: 'Whereas it is a most common and Usual course for many to send their Daughters to common Schools to be taught together with and amongst all sorts of Youths, which course is by many conceived very uncomely and not decent therefore the said School Master may not admit any of that Sex to be taught in the said School.'

The endowed School was still exclusively for boys 'who have attained the age of 8' according to a Visitation enquiry of 1838, with some girls attending Dame schools. Thomas Hughes, himself Rugby- and Oxford-educated, perpetuated the patronizing concept of ill-educated girls by portraying his young Tom Brown pitting his precocious wit and cunning against scatty, clumsy Charity Lamb – a

Tom Brown's School is now a local museum with a fine collection of Thomas Hughes' work amid the local history of Uffington

dull (though decent) girl from the village school trained by Madam Brown in the duties of nurserymaid. 'Our hero', meanwhile, is encouraged to bulldoze his oafish way 'on his little Shetland into the cottage and round the table, where the old dame and her pupils were seated at their work'; and the author allowed himself another jibe at the Fairer Sex acquiring education by blaming it for social divisions in the old order of village life, because it led to 'farmers' daughters caring more to make bad foreign music than good English cheeses'.

A girls' National School was built in 1851 by voluntary subscription and a government grant, and become the Uffington National School with an infants' school added in 1872, by which date the Thomas Saunders endowed boys' school was in a dilapidated condition quite unsuitable for educational purposes.

The old school, where Tom Brown and Jacob Doodle-calf loitered in the porch to delight the boys and vex the master, was sold for £35 and the money applied 'without authority' to the building additions of the National School. Remodelled and modernised, and now of Controlled status, Uffington still has an attractive village school.

A statute made in the 'High Court of Parliament', 27 October 1598, enquired 'into deceits and breaches of trust concerning lands, tenements and other specified gifts to any charitable uses outlined and declared by the Commission'. The Commission for Pious Uses acted as a watchdog over the assets donated to charitable purposes, and Inquisitions were held during the next century in various places to check on the affairs of the parish. Such Inquisitions have proved valuable in tracing educational bequests.

Laughton-en-le-Morthen, near Sheffield, can also date its village school as a contemporary with Tom Brown's from an Inquisition held in Doncaster when Anthony Eyre gave a piece of land 5 yds. × 10 yds. 'for use of a school', and Edmund Laughton (the Elder) gave an adjoining one quarter of a decayed homestead. The intent of the trustees was that 'the school house should for ever be kept, used and employed as a common school for the learning and instruction in learning of the children of the inhabitants of Laughton-en-le-Morthen'. The vicar gave land nearby, on which a house was built about 1668 for the use of the headmaster 'for ever after' on condition that he paid four shillings to four poor widows every year. Rents from other land left by another benefactor was for an annual salary to the master of £3 6s. 8d.

A further Inquisition of 1789 revealed that the school was in a state of 'ruin and decay' – the trustees had long since died and their 'heirs male' to whom the terms had been entrusted had obviously relinquished their responsibilities. The Charity Commissioners drew up a constitution aimed at securing a continuance of the trust body and conditions by which the master were bound to the trustees, but despite their efforts the school appeared similarly neglected by 1820. Not surprisingly, the welfare and administration of the village school must have seemed but of trivial concern to a body of local worthies at a time of the Napoleonic Wars, followed by the national unrest which swept in with the agricultural depression. On the indenture of 1820 is a notice of conveyance from Edmund Laughton of Tickhill, a surviving descendant of the early benefactor who was declared to be the legal possessor of the Trust property, to Anthony Butler St Leger for 'ten shillings of legal money'.

Much of the original 1610-19 building still stands cornering the road facing the parish church. Lovely old stone mullion windows, discrete and dignified, show their mellowed age, with what was originally the master's living quarters above. Sharper cut outlines of the stone mullions of the windows in the furthest end identify it as the extension built with the government grant 200 years later. For some local political reason, records speak of the boys' school as endowed, with the girls' school and Sunday School 'supported by public subscription' – although the original bequest was for 'children' in a co-educational sense. It is a focal point to which the neighbours go to community functions. Listed in the Wase Returns, compiled in the mid-seventeenth century, as a Grammar School, All Saints' C. of E. (Aided) School is probably the oldest survivor of an early endowed school in Yorkshire.

The history of educational endowments is written in the ancient acres of the fields and meadows of Britain, for something like sixty per cent of the income was derived from rents from investments 'lade out on land'. Their names must have tripped off the tongue of the poor for whose benefit they were intended, like a medieval liturgy:

> Bean lands and Swan Fields in nearby Lechlade financed Lady Mico's Charity for apprenticing four poor boys of the Parish of Fairford; Old Woman's Leaze, Hickwalkers and Four Patches were among those at Wotton-under-Edge.

The land given by the FitzGerald family to build the red-brick village school at Naseby in Northamptonshire, is tied to the conditions that it is for as long as the school remains a school. Land was considered a sound investment as it increased in value, and some village schools actually benefited by the enclosures. Enclosure at Duntisbourne Abbots doubled the income for Sapperton School; but St Chloe's School, across the valley lost two acres when the turnpike road was widened and straightened between Nailsworth to Stroud – compensation was eventually hard won. But the worst disaster to charity lands in Gloucestershire was in 1815 when extraordinary autumn tidal waves breached the sea wall and flooded the lands of the Anthony Edmonds School on the Severn estuary. The school trustees were liable under the Law of Sewers to repair the wall, and were forced to close the school and mortgage the lands to pay the costs.

Reference in 1830 to a sum of five pounds for the educating of five poor children to be discontinued, and a proposal to shut up the schoolroom at the church, left the village of Appledore in Kent without a school until 1840 when the Revd F. Goold spearheaded a fund by preaching a fervent and rhetorical sermon which raised an incredible £29. A room was rented from a Mr Adams and in 1847 half an acre of land on the Heath was conveyed from the Dean and Chapter of Canterbury, the Lords of Appledore Manor. In 1848 'Paine' was paid half-a-crown for trees for the school, and two men, a horse and cart moving earth to the school cost six shillings. The school was extended in 1875 and has remained little altered ever since.

Educating the poor often took quaint and curious forms; in many villages it was the teacher who was endowed with a fixed stipend made by benefactors with an extraordinary faith in eternity and total ignorance of eventual inflation.

In 1680, William Oldisworth left provision for 'a poor School Dame to be paid one shilling a quarter during the term of 1,800 years (and upwards) to hear four poor boys of Fairford at her house read one chapter between them all and repeat the Church Catechism among them all on every Sunday at one of the clock; and also six shillings and sixpence be paid at the end of every of the said quarters to a Baker there successively that shall send on every Saturday therein six penny loaves of good wheaten bread to be divided among them'. Any boy that failed to read and repeat satisfactorily had to forfeit his loaf – which was divided between those 'that did read and repeat' – *after* the Dame had taken half.

The noble dames who founded so many of our village schools were usually far more explicit in their idea of the curriculum than their male counterparts. Elizabeth Farmor at Fairford specified in her Will of 1704 that the boys of the endowed school should 'read English well and also to write a good legible hand'; Mary Barker, her aunt and co-foundress, specified that her money should be 'laid out in books proper for learning them to read and write and to buy each and every of them as they shall attain the years of Discretion, a Bible and the Whole Duty of Man'. Lady Jane Mico, great aunt of Elizabeth Farmor, founded an apprenticeship charity in 1670 with indentures, although varying in their binding on different crafts contained a common clause for elementary education: 'to read the English tongue and to write and cast accounts sufficient for a person of the trade'. Apprenticeships varied from seven to seventeen years' service, during which time the apprentice was not to 'haunt alehouses, not play dice nor cards nor enter into matrimony'. A 'good new suit for Holy Days', physic and surgery (except in the case of the small pox), a Prayer Book and Testament, were also provided by the endowment which lasted as an apprentice charity for 200 years, to be finally amalgamated with the endowments of her niece and great niece for the benefit of Farmor's School.

Apprenticeships offered some form of education as well as training before schools were built specifically for the purpose. In the case of 'charity children' they were almost inevitable, as the Overseers of the Poor would be anxious to remove the cost of providing relief from a heavily burdened parish.

Casting accounts and making children 'better capable of trade and calling for gaining their livelihoods' was usually the privilege of the boys. The only addition to the monotony of reading, writing and scripture for the girls was needlework (favoured only after it was a testable subject for earning a grant under the Revised Code), spinning or 'marking plain work'.

Elizabeth Denward, wife of the rector, gave very precise instructions for the Stelling Minnis School which she founded in 1784. With remarkable foresight for the age, she included girls' education in her endowment and the salary for a schoolmistress –

although the mistress was only paid £6 a year whereas the master received £20. School houses, with meadows for the use of the master and mistress, were also provided by the trust funds. Any remaining income was to be spent on two chaldrons of coal each year for use in the schoolrooms, on hats and greatcoats, books, necessities and repairs. Any deficit was to be met by lessening the number of children, the teacher's salary or the number of greatcoats given.

Husbandry of some kind – 'gardening, hedging, griping' – was also included in the curriculum decreed by the foundress of the school. Agriculture and hop-picking affected the attendances, as in other rural areas, and even coloured the comments of the Diocesan Inspector who reported in 1852 that 'perhaps the manners of the boys admit a little more cultivation'.

Today, fewer children come from agricultural backgrounds, yet when Elizabeth Denward stipulated in 1784 that the children should be instructed in reading, writing and arithmetic with the girls 'working with the needle at plain work', she might well have been gratified to know that in 1984 pupils were writing: 'I like school because I like reading. The best thing I like is maths. I think school is great. It teaches you things you'll need when you grow up. You'll need sewing when you grow up. We do that!'

The village of Ardeley in Hertfordshire was, until 1854, Yardley – so famed for its malt that the clergy of St Paul's Cathedral (to whom the parish regularly supplied it) funded the building of the Church of St Lawrence across the thatched cottage edged green. The village school was built in 1835 on glebe land adjoining the churchyard, adopted the name of the church and maintains a close Christian ethos; the statue of St Lawrence on the wall of the north aisle was funded mainly by the pupils in 1962.

The names of the subscribers who financed the building of the school at Willoughby-on-the-Wolds are acknowledged on a large board, still in its original position. In the Leicestershire border parish of Claybrooke Parva the village school, built in 1813, stands as a memorial to the local benefactor Mark Smith. Temperance Gell founded the school at Derbyshire's Carsington in 1726 for twenty poor children of Carson and Hopton to read, write 'and other proper works', according to the plaque above the school door.

Paradoxically, many clothiers, whose industry proved a counter-attraction to school, set up generous educational endowments. In the Cotswold cloth country, the largest endowment (of £6,000) was left by Sir Thomas Rich in 1666 to found one of the rare boarding schools or 'hospitals' for poor children.

Founded on the principles of Christ's Hospital, London, Sir Thomas Rich's Hospital at Gloucester wore the Blue Coat until 1882. They formed part of the Mayor's procession to the Cathedral

A schoolroom scene in stained glass at St Loes, Amberley

and allowed to eat the remnants of the Audit Feast. The name, not the principles, still lives on as one of Gloucestershire's oldest schools.

Dick Whittington is a legend, not a myth; and a later member of his family endowed a school at Cold Ashton near Bath in 1715. Nathanial Hicks left a rent-charge of £5 a year for a Dissenting School at Cam in 1728.

Nathanial Cambridge, a rich merchant left £1,000 to found the St Chloe School at Amberley. Part of the legacy had been received from his 'Honord Aunte Tooke' – a remarkable woman who figured large in the Civil War as her husband violated the local vicarages when leading his Parliamentarian army in the siege of Gloucester, while her father entertained Charles I at their family home. One condition of the will was 'to keep at school six boys, to be taught to read English and to write and cast accounts'.

Possibly unique in the subject of stained-glass windows, is a schoolroom scene, painted for St Loes by Edward Payne who had lived there with his father, also a celebrated stained-glass artist. Henry Payne, a student of Christopher Whall, was attracted to St Loes by William Morris's view of it as the ideal house. Following the tradition of the medieval artist as storyteller, Edward Payne illustrated the history of the house in the two-panelled window. 'Syngt-Lee originally a Roman Brickfield. Later given by the Culverhouse family as a Resthouse for the Abbey of Malmesbury' appears at the top of the right-hand light. A Benedictine monk rests from his labours in the herb garden as work is going on to extend the house in the background. A farmer and his wife in Stuart dress share a horse and the bottom panel with farmworkers and the headless ghost of the lady who walks the packhorse track behind St Loes.

The second light bears a top panel which states 'in 1699 Nathaniel Cambridge of Hamborough gave £1,000 for educating the Poor Boys of Woodchester and Rodborough, with which money Saint-Loe Farm was purchased'. A schoolroom in which the master, with a book held behind his back, dominates the main panel, and is completed by a picture of the artist's father at work at his easel, depicting his years at St Loes. The boys and the usher slept in the attic rooms, with windows in the roof overlooking the lovely countryside. Punishment for telling lies was a dousing under the courtyard pump where the boys had their mouths 'washed clean'. It was Henry Payne who wrote verses 27 and 28 from Chapter 12 of Ezekiel on the jutting dormer of the school clock high on the Cotswold stone roof. The school has been a private house for many years now.

A mercer at Painswick, still in the Stroud Valley, left a school fund on the condition that the parish raised an equal amount. Closely resembling the Gloucestershire stone-built villages is Chipping in Lancashire – the old English name for 'market'. Chipping also grew up on the wool industry and many of its fine stone buildings date from the seventeenth century when trade was at its peak. John Brabin, a local dyer and wool merchant and bachelor, 'being infirme of body' left money to build a school and funds to relieve the poor. The school still stands at the end of cobbled Windy Street, neighbour to a row of almshouses. The carved stone finials on the homely porch sets apart the one from the other. The old school in the centre of the village served its original purpose from 1684 until new larger premises were built in 1880. Brabins School, which still benefits from the endowments of John Brabin's will, perpetuates its founder's name, and the old school is still used by the community as a Sunday School and youth club.

Still serving the youth, as a Girl Guides' and Brownies' hall, is the old Victorian school at Linby, where the river divides as it runs through the Nottinghamshire village. A new school, in the Clasp style of the Sixties, was built some hundred yards distant and exercises the judgement of staff and pupils alike as they try to fit its name into regulated spaces; for now it incorporates the school from the neighbouring village and has the delightful title of Linby-cum-Papplewick.

The school charities which survived the longest are those where trusteeship was chosen with continuity in the mind of the benefactor at the outset. The parish clergy and churchwardens or overseers were a natural and usually safe bet. The impressive list of trustees of the village school at Marshfield, founded by Mrs Dionysia Long, were headed by none other than the Bishop of Gloucester.

Most trustees were of the English middle class, expected to fulfil their duties free for the benefit of the lower classes. Exceptionally, expenses were allowed if the conditions of the ward seemed particularly onerous and we find that George Townsend decreed that the body entrusted with five schools in the north Cotswolds should after their meeting on the first Saturday in May each year, 'have an eightpenny ordinary', with five shillings for beer after dinner and a pair of gloves each 'not to exceed twelve-pence'.

ARCHITECTURAL STYLES, SITING AND REGIONAL DIFFERENCES

It is the interesting old village and the forty-five-acre bird-haunted reedy mere, at the end of which it shelters and slopes among the woods to the north, which combined gave their names to the Hanmer family – and through them to Hanmer village school.

Secluded at the end of a narrow lane is Hanmer School, the oldest in the Maelor, it was built in 1676 according to the diaries of a Philip Henry who was in charge of the parish of Worthenbury but 'given to Puritanism'. Parish registers contain the names of a high proportion of Hanmer people with academic degrees, some of whom were listed as schoolmasters many years before the school was built, so classes were probably held, as was the custom in other places, in the church. The idea of building a school obviously met with local approval, but it was still some fifty-two years after a Roger Billings left his 100 marks for that purpose that the single room school was built.

In common with the elaborate timber-framing of seventeenth-century buildings of the wooded English-Welsh border styles, Hanmer School has a fair amount of timber in its original construction. This is detailed in the accounts for building the school house, and attracted the attention of generations of the village schoolchildren who have gazed on the massive black beams supporting the roof of what is now the Infant classroom. And no doubt delight in finding that one of the craftsmen of old made a mistake by putting one of the main cross beam balustrades upside down.

The accounts gave a fascinating insight of both quantity and costs involved as well as who were the local tradesmen and the irregularities of the spelling in 1676.

THE ACCOUNTS FOR BUILDING THE SCHOOL HOUSE AT HANMER

	£	s	d
James Higginbotham for making 50,000 bricks at 3s 10d ye thousand	9	11	8
Jonathan Cliffe for coale slacke	4	14	0
Thomas Young for wood to burn ye bricks		4	6
Edward Allert for falling and squaring ye timber at Kenwick	9	0	0
Jonathan Cliffe for slates (10,000) and carriage	9	0	0
For carrying water for ye bricks		2	10
For making up ye brick kiln with sods			10
Mr Owen Barton for timber	8	10	0
For 206 measures of lime	4	6	0
Ye bricklayer	6	10	0
Edward Allert the carpenter	3	0	0
Spent on ye workmen at several times		2	11
For digging foundation and making sawpit		2	8
For 2 roods and a half more timber and sawing	3	7	0
For 3 casements dubble	2	6	0
For ropes for scaffoldings poles and boards		13	0
For ye carriage of bricks sand and lats	2	5	0
For use of a bench to John Corberly		1	4
For a basket			2
Roger Done for iron work		2	6
For lime for ye covering		11	7
Richard Jennings for slating	3	16	1
For 2,000 more slates	1	14	0
For 4 dozen of crests and carriage		11	6
For nails to Andrew Mainwaring	1	1	2

	£	s	d
For 1,700 of lats		19	10
More lime fore plastering up ye school and windows	1	1	6
Thomas Statham for plastering ye windows		17	10
For 34 feet of ½ inch boards for ye desks		4	2
For making and hanging ye doors		2	6
For 100 of nails			4
For haire at several times		4	8
For a pair of hinges for ye door		3	0
Thomas Evans for plastering and beame filling	1	4	0
Gave his son a birrage			6
Thomas Evans for filling and laying ye floor	1	0	0
John Broockfield for a chair		2	6
For ye boards for ye doore			2
For boards and a writing deske		5	0
For half hundred of dubble spikes and small nails			5
Timber to be form posts 4 feet long in alle		4	0
Total	£71	7	1

The subscribers included a John Eddowe of London (formerly of Manchester) who had been a scholar at Hanmer. The total subscriptions were recorded as £71 7s. One penny short of the total cost! Perhaps this was what necessitated the donations in kind to complete the school, listed as:

John Beddowe of Tybroughton gentleman did glase the school house in Hanmer at his own cost which came to £3 0 0. Richard Heath of Tybroughton, Humphrey Beddow and Owen Powell of Halghton did jointly bench and desk the said school £1 4s. Thomas Yates of Whitechurch gentleman gave nails and a lock and boards for ye schools house door 10s.

The rules for the new school were drawn up on 31 May 1676 by the feoffes:

I 20 scholars to be taught by the teacher.

II The wages from the lowest to the highest to be the same, viz. one shilling and sixpence the quarter and noe more except for such as write they to pay 2 shillings the quarter.

III Poor and rich alike to pay one shilling entrance and noe more to be demanded.

IV One of the feoffes was to be the treasurer each year and to admit poor scholars at the concent of the minister.

V If any poor boy was admitted and was absent for 20 consecutive days without permission of the minister and the feoffe another was to be admitted in his place.

VI Strangers for entrance and wages are left to the masters discretion.

After such explicit records there is a long silence during which the school had obviously deteriorated as, according to the Charity Commissioner's Report of 1847, 'the building was damp and badly drained ... the furniture was rotting and everywhere was dirty ... I could find no decent place to lay my papers.' Again, it was local support which righted matters; £100 was raised and school was held in a room above Humphrey Hanmer's boathouse at Merehead while repairs were carried out on the school building. A playground was added in 1861 and ten years later a girls school was built, with a school house. Further extensions and improvements were made in 1894, but at the centre still remains –

HAEC SCHOLA AD MDCLXXVI DEO GLORIA

Somerset's Lovington village school has its foundations rooted in the end of the seventeenth century, when a family known as the Mary Marys survived abject poverty by aggressive defence. Mary Mary, the daughter of the village cobbler, was only 16 when her parents died. Mary Mary cared not only for her four younger brothers and sisters but as many of the village's other orphaned children as she could. They formed a formidable gang living by stealing what they could from the villagers and the travellers who passed along the turnpike or stopped at the inn on the edge of the Common, chasing off children from neighbouring villages if they entered Lovington begging for bread.

The education of these unholy terrors into more civilised ways was the subject of Parson Connock's sermons, but it was a local farmer of humble means whose own children had all died in infancy who practised what the parson preached. Farmer John Whitehead willed the rents of nine acres of pasture land at Foddington to be used for the schooling of the 'poor children of Lovington for ever'.

In 1716 seven poor children attended Lovington's first school, probably in Widow James's own cottage, where they were taught to read and pray and sew. The idea of a village school started to attract more children and at one time the Parish Clerk took over as schoolmaster. Following complaints from neighbouring villages, the Royal Commission investigated the charity funds and the Trustees took steps to make Lovingon into a proper school. In 1845 Lovington became a National School and children were allowed to attend from Wheathill, Hornblotton and Alford. The school, with its attached house now forming part of it, is a listed building and names of people connected with its early history are kept alive as the names of the school sports teams.

Is not all my charge done for the good benefit of you and posterity, your parrish and the country round aboute you, and will not this be a liveing benediction of posterity to you, and yours, and all aboute you?

Sir John Moore, 1696

Sir John Moore School at Appleby Magna, from an 'improved' design of Christopher Wren

A year later Sir John Moore built the school which bears his name at a cost of £2,393 for the village of Appleby Magna in Leicestershire. Of an ancient local family who made a fortune in the East India trade, Sir John became Lord Mayor of London and chose no less an architect than Sir Christopher Wren to design his village school! What is attributed as Wren's original plan is now at All Souls' College, Oxford – a simple classic design which was 'improved upon' by a Leicester architect and sculptor, William Wilson.

Grandiose by village school style, the imposing building was designed to house two schools, each with its own autonomy. The Headmaster of the Grammar School lived in the house on the west side and received £65 a year; the Headmaster of the English, or Free School, lived on the east side and was paid £45 a year. The boys of each school were not allowed to mix. In 1904 the Grammar School closed and the building was used as the Boys National School until 1933. Subsequent conversion by the governing body – on whose Board members of the Moore family have always served – has given Appleby Magna a Church of England (Aided) village school of remarkable architectural merit and outstanding beauty. Its other claim to historical note is that one old boy, Sir William Huskisson – Secretary to the Board of Trade – was the first person in the world to be killed by a train.

Whippingham village school in the Isle of Wight, has the distinction of being designed by Prince Albert, the Prince Consort, built in the 1860s on land donated by Queen Victoria. Except for a small recent extension, the school architecturally remains unchanged and is part of the island's Victorian heritage. Queen Victoria took an active interest in the school and visited it frequently. When spending Christmas holidays at Osborne House, the Queen presented a fairy doll to the 'best behaved girl in the school', and when the London choirboys went to Osborne House for the royal wedding they camped at the village school.

Founded in 1704, Clyst St George must have one of Devon's oldest village schools. The rebuilding of 1859 retained the near monastic style with wood and wrought-iron cloisters to produce a most remarkable school building, under the talented and outstanding rector, the Revd Henry Thomas Ellacombe who had worked under Brunel as a gifted civil engineer before his ordination.

Of all the twin villages in the Cotswolds, Eastleach Turville and Martin present the most fascinating study of parish politics. Separated by the shallow Leach, each has its church and once had its own school and until they were amalgamated in 1935 were separate parishes, on occasion having to request that one should refrain from burying their dead in the other's churchyard. A single school for the two Eastleaches had been started by 1818 but in 1826 they had their own in Union with the National Society and were supported by John Keble who was then curate of St Martin's Church. The clapper bridge linking the two villages over the Leach is named Keble Bridge after the poet, and it is claimed that of his many hymns, at least 'Sun of My Soul' was written here. In 1863 a National School to serve both Eastleaches was built at Martin by voluntary subscriptions and labour, the villagers themselves digging the foundations. From a school roll of 90 in 1885, it had but 9 in 1974 – the school closed and the children transferred to Southrop.

Labouring under two names for four and a half centuries, the tiny Cotswold village, which was simply Aston in medieval times, was officially designated as Cold Aston or Aston Blank. Records speak of Aston being Cold at least by 1255 and Blank from 1535, and since then both names have been used impartially to the great confusion of everyone except the villagers. For years they had regarded it as Cold Aston, but the county and district councils, the Inland Revenue and the Ordnance Survey insisted it was Aston Blank, despite the Post Office stating it was not Blank but Cold!

The Parish Council applied under the 1933 Local Government Act to finalise the matter and the village became officially Cold Aston in 1972; the Ordnance Survey finally agreed to change the name on their maps, but the signposts still carry both names!

Aston Blank School became Cold Aston School to conform with the single identity – but the school records carry the dual names and show that a school was established by the Lord of the Manor for ten poor children in the early eighteenth century. A parochial return of 1846

Casual and colourful at Cold Aston

states that Aston Blank had a Sunday School for twenty children, but a day school was needed and the vicar 'expected' H. F. Hope, Esquire, Lord of the Manor, to build one – which he did. Opened in 1861 and privately owned by Mrs Hope, the school carried on as a church school from 1879 to qualify for the annual grant aid, as it was then recognised by the National Society (and the Government) as a public elementary school. The schoolroom was under the same roof as the house, and its only other function was as a Sunday School.

In 1910 the school had sixty-four pupils, aged four to fourteen, in the one classroom. The Inspectors recommended that a second classroom be built. It was not, but a cloakroom was – heavily financed by farmers from the neighbouring village of Notgrove. Notgrove requested that a proposed new school be built there, this was refused by the Local Education Authority who then built a new classroom (not a school) at Aston in 1914. On the closure of Turkdean School the catchment area matched the ecclesiastic parish, and the school enlarged by taking in the master's house.

Tunstall in Kent acquired its village school from the Rector, the Revd George Bridges Moore, who made a foundation for the education of the children of his employees. Originally known as the

Rectory School, the lattice-windowed flint-faced school building with its steeply-pitched roof and tall chimneys was built in 1846 and given to the parish by three of his children and still maintains strong Church of England ties and principles.

'Yesterday morning the infant school was opened. It is very infant indeed, only about eight children, the eldest six', wrote Ida Farrer of the school built by her husband in 1873 at Abinger Hammer. One of the oldest villages in England, Abinger acquired its 'Hammer' for its hamlet in the valley from the iron-forging hammer powered by the pretty stream in the sixteenth century – one of the last places in Surrey where the industry lingered longer.

Alternative schools: No transport will be provided, since both are within two miles. Share involves a walk beside the dangerous A25, or an expensive and inconvenient bus ride. It also means going on to Middle School in Guildford Borough Abinger, in Mole Valley District, looks towards Dorking. Abinger Common is almost two miles along narrow, hilly country lanes, and there is no public transport. Our school was started because the Common (school started 1865) was too far for Hammer children. The advent of the motor car (for those many still without one) increased the dangers.

Abinger Hammer Village School Trust Appeal, 1982

The case for keeping the school open today argues as strongly on the same geographical basis as did that for opening it or limiting it to children of the scattered village area a hundred years ago.

12 June 1883 The children who attend (the Abinger schools) live at long distances scattered far apart over a great extent of common and fir woods, and it is quite impossible that they can attend in rough weather. There is no village near the Abinger Upper School.

Minute Book

Lady Modiford's School at Walkhampton was founded in 1719 as an endowed charity school limited to '20 boys and no more at any one time, inhabiting within the said parish of Walkhampton'. A cottage, thought to have been on the site of the present school, was for the use of the schoolmaster to teach his scholars, with provision for the erection of a new schoolhouse if the cottage was found to be unsuitable. The Trustees paid out of parts of the rents and profits of the premises £17 per annum to the schoolmaster 'for teaching of boys in the space of four years, to read, write and cast accounts, and for instructing them in the Church of England catechism'.

It was not until 1785 that girls were admitted and a 'school mistress appointed when Mrs Shillibeer taught 10 girls'.

The foresight of Lady Modiford, whose family were the successors of Drake – of Armada fame – to the local estates, enabled development of the school in its early building with its attractive clock tower centrepiece with scope to extend both structurally and educationally. Now a co-educational Primary School of 'aided' status, the school buildings are still owned by the Trustees of the charity and the Governors have a greater influence on the teaching of Religious Education and staff appointments than their counterparts in county and 'controlled' schools. Lady Modiford founded a similar school at Buckland Monachorum and her younger daughter, Madam Mary Dean later established a school bearing her own name at Tamerton Foliot – all three schools have continued without a break to the present time.

Lady Katherine Leveson founded the school which still bears her name in Temple Balsall, originally the base of the Knights Templar. School started here as early as 1694; the present Victorian building has modern extensions architecturally in keeping.

The Wordsworths' words captured the timeless charm of Hawkshead in Cumbria; William in his poetry, Dorothy in her journals. The village retains its heart of cobbles, tangle of narrow streets, cottages up steps and its village school. Rebuilt since it was founded in 1585 by Edwin Sandys, a local man who became Archbishop of York, the school where the young William went at the age of eight has its original desks – including the one on which Wordsworth cut his name – quaint chimneys like upturned tubs, and an old sundial above the door.

Caerwent's links with the past are robust rather than romantic. This Gwent village must be one of the most remarkable in the kingdom, being still enclosed by walls built some 1,700 years ago when little Welsh Caerwent was the thriving Roman town of Venta Silurum. The Victorian-built village school stands solidly on the old Roman site and survived the threat of closure in 1984.

The planner's pen has destroyed where the sea failed at Penclawdd. Since it was built in 1875, the little stone school has withstood the tidal floods which threatened its existence because it was below sea-level – the same waters have borne in the livelihood of the village for centuries, for here on the broad Loughor Estuary are the famous cockle-women who ride out at low tide on horse-drawn carts to collect the harvest from the sea.

Drayton Parslow in Buckinghamshire is one of the few villages to have withstood the redistribution and detribalisation suffered by so many in this age of shifting populace and alternate sources of employment. Equidistant from the western extremity of the designated area of Milton Keynes, Newton Longville and Stewkley, Mursley and Stoke Hammond, the majority of the village is still home-based despite a changing agricultural scene. The extraordinary complexity of its inter-related families featured in the Radio 4 programme *This Island Now*, and occupied a half page of the *Sunday Times* in March 1971. Forty-one per cent of the householders were born in the village and eight out of every ten households have a direct personal link with the village school, which has served the whole community without sectarian or class distinction since 1878.

True to tradition of country-bred self-sufficiency, Drayton Parslow founded its own school independent of the church by selling the Poor Law cottages 'for the permanent advantage of this parish' on a site offered them at an affordable sum by Lord Carrington, and was maintained out of local rates. The School Board strongly condemned the 1902 Education Bill on the grounds that 'the County Council cannot deal with the question like the popular Elected men on the spot'.

Dodford, knotted in a tangle of winding Worcestershire lanes, illustrates a particularly fascinating facet of how an individual community coped with drastic social reform. Dodford, in itself, is interesting by differing from the usual physical form of the traditional village. The church, usually the oldest building of the village around which others radiate, was not built until 1908, so Dodford did not become an independent parish until this century, and this has accounted for its meandering shape.

Against a background of abject poverty, brought about by the industrial revolution which forced the cottage nailmasters into hard competition by lowered wages, a School Board was finally elected after fierce political debate and an abortive attempt to avoid an election by a private settlement. Earlier attempts to bring education to the children of Dodford's poor had been met in part by the Vicar of Bromsgrove walking out there 'on an errand of Mercy' armed with Bible and chalk after conducting three services on a Sunday. By 1863 a Mission Hall was built. Sunday School was also available for the non-conformists when the Baptist Chapel was opened two years later. But weekly lessons of a mere couple of hours divided between reading, writing and the Scriptures fell a long way short of the educational needs, and when Dodford School opened in 1877 two-thirds of the children between the ages of five and thirteen did not know the alphabet. The Chartists were rather better catered for and their educational efforts were commended in the Worcestershire Chronicle.

Although recognising the need for a school, many parents were reluctant to lose another wage-earner from the cottage forge or farm, especially as they were expected to pay for it – 2d a week for infants and 3d for the first and second classes. As it turned out, the fee had to be remitted in the first few months of the school's opening; the furniture had not arrived, and when it did the children did not, partly due to an extended strike of the nailers, who resolutely survived on 'cold tater water and half a pint of fourpenny', and partly due to the scattered catchment area – living two miles away from the school was a reasonable excuse for not attending, and it was recorded that not one child came from Timberhanger. A further attempt to ensure full attendance was made when the Board resolved that the holidays 'should include a month or so about midsummer as to include a convenient season for the strawberry picking'.

A totally different village from the rural idyll is that of Wollescote. Notwithstanding its proximity the Lye – which Sir Cedric Hardwicke (who was born there in 1893) described as 'allegedly, there was no more uncouth corner on the map of England ... the town earned its living in the sprawling South Staffordshire coalfield, making anvils, bathtubs and iron buckets. This was a world made hideous by foundries and blast furnaces belching out smoke, flames and soot by day and night', Wollescote is still regarded as a village.

The contiguity of Lye and Wollescote has been and is such that they are historically bounded together, and the names are to be found in partnership when it comes to looking at early school foundations. In consequence, it is against the background of Lye that we look at Wollescote. But a century ago, Lye was found by its vicar to be 'a poor looking place – a place many would have called squalid. The mud huts were very much in evidence then. The people built them themselves, the boys throwing up balls of mud to the father as he built or repaired the walls'. In common with the general feeling of the Black Country, education received but tardy recognition of its value to the children, weighed against the loss of their earnings so vital to the poor family's meagre income when boys and girls at 10 or 11 were striving to become skilled nail-makers – an achievement reckoned by whether or not they could make 1,000 nails a day, for which they would receive 5¼ pence for every 1,200.

Wollescote maintained its independence as a separate parish until 1897. Against hostile prejudices, mistrust and antagonism, the Wollescote School opened in 1882 with fifty-seven pupils, aged between seven and thirteen under the charge of Major Pardoe, a local lad who had qualified through the monitorial system to become head and, initially, the sole teacher – and a figurehead in the school's history. A strict disciplinarian, who was but nine years older than his oldest pupil when he started his career as headteacher, he would line the boys up every morning for an inspection with the thoroughness of a military parade – although aptly named in the circumstance, Major was one of the names borrowed from the impressive social ranks of Earl, Major and Squire favoured for Christian names in the area of the time. 'Cleanliness is next to Godliness' was one of his maxims, and at his own expense he provided towels, brushes and soap to raise the standard of his often destitute and dirty pupils. Such was the respect in which generations of his pupils held him that they stood to attention to salute him in the street when they were fathers themselves, and even grandfathers.

Saluting the Headmaster and curtseying to the lady teachers is a custom which persisted right into the 1960s at Great Haywood in Staffordshire. Staunchly and almost wholly Catholic, the parish of St John the Baptist nucleated around the old faith of the landed gentry – their retainers and tenants being chosen or preferred initially for their religious persuasion.

It was for the children of the Catholic community that education first took root in Great Haywood in the back of the church which had removed stone by stone from Tixall in 1845; many of the numbers on the stones to aid the rebuilding are still to be seen. In 1855, under the care of Father Benjamin Butland, St John's Roman Catholic School was built for the village. The building was replaced in the Sixties, but it still retains its name and very pronounced family atmosphere.

William Penn School, in the small West Sussex village of Coolham, acquired its notable name only as recently as 1973, when the village school moved to a new building. Its foundation dates to 1891 to the Society of Friends, who had been active in the area since the mid-seventeenth century. The Quaker movement influenced and encouraged William Penn who lived at Warminghurst. The Blue Idol has served as the Society's Meeting House since 1682 to the present day and the old school building near the village centre was used for Gospel meetings on Sundays. The Round House, an old turnpike cottage, adjacent to the school accommodated the staff, but was demolished in an extension and modernisation programme in 1914.

Even in this century the occasional village school has been built in the tradition of the early philanthropists. The Depression of the Thirties hit hard at the Tyneside area but spearheaded by Commander Vyner, who formed the Fountains Abbey Trust, the Swarland Estate – owned by the Shilbottle Colliery – was purchased to which unemployed couples with at least two children were invited to settle and create a new community.

Each house had an acre-and-a-half to support the family; fruit trees, chickens and a pig – the latter housed in a communal piggery – were provided. A twenty-five-year interest free mortgage rent of 6s 6d was offered, with full ownership at the end of that period and all previously incurred debts settled. Employment was available at the specially built tweed mill, a saw mill and a brick works – the latter still a thriving business, but now in private ownership. Many young men went into the Navy – no doubt influenced by Commander Vyner's naval career, and the 'big house' attracted girls into local domestic service.

As the settlement's population increased and overcrowded the small

Swarland School in the 1980s

village school a mile away at Newton on the Moor, it was Commander Vyner who arranged for Swarland to have its own village school. It opened on 29 November 1937 with 133 pupils drawn from the settlement itself and the immediate area.

The outbreak of war took many families back to the town and drew the men away for active service. The local employment situation changed at the end of the war and the return of a Labour Government in 1947 marked the end of the Settlers Society. The houses were purchased by those families who wished to remain, others sold theirs and moved away. Despite the initial changes and its youth, Swarland has settled as a village community, and the village school has all the inherent character and human characteristics of village schools twice its age. Even the eccentricities peculiar only to school plumbing seem to have been built into the new school for the earliest entries in the Log Book show the Headteacher, who transferred to Swarland from Newton on the Moor, 'inspecting the lavatories' every few days; then the fires smoked and soot floated through the classrooms.

Pupils, like plumbing, change but little.

25 Feb. 1938	Thomas Lough, 12½ years, because of repeated talking, after having been spoken to several times has been sent home at 10.30. His attendance has been cancelled.

17 June 1938 — Alan Fisher, 13½ years, stuck a dart in William Riddell's neck during the dinner hour. The wound was very slight, a prick, but he was sent home in Fisher's care. The children have been lectured on the seriousness of such behaviour.

And in that special way of school reports, the teacher's and the pupil's versions are totally in variance between what appears to have happened and what the boys themselves know to have happened: the one is recorded for all time; the other – a secret shared between school friends standing the test of time. As they recall it over a half century later, it was while they were playing cricket that Tommy (the chatterbox of the February entry) 'bowled' a dart at Alan – who batted it and Billy 'failed to get out of the way'. Pleased to be excused school, the aggrieved and aggressor played about until home time with neither parents nor teacher any the wiser.

8 Mar. 1962 — Mr Braham, County Chief Inspector, visited to discuss the temporary nature of the school. Its present life expectancy is about 3 years.

Mrs Rita Gleghorn, the present headteacher, turns back the pages of the Log Book to that entry which her father made a quarter of a century ago!

Cuckney School has a longer history in education than the foundation of the school itself. The parish nudges Derbyshire but the village grew up on its Nottinghamshire cotton industry. Of the three mills built on the River Poulter, only one now remains and that has been Cuckney village school since 1848.

Upper Mill was built in 1785 by William Toplis at the far end of the village, away from the parish church and the historic Greendale Oak inn, to make use of the old forge dam to provide water power for his worsted spinning manufactory. Having leased the land from Lord Bathurst, the principal landowner in the parish, and built his three-storey mill, William Toplis and Son started their worsted – and later cotton – spinning on Arkwright's principles – but with child labour. The Toplis family had 'an arrangement' with the London Foundling Hospital and between 1786 and 1805 no fewer than 782 children were registered as apprentices of the mill.

The Apprentices Register recorded the children's names, the date they were received, their age, the parish from which they came, by whom they were sent, the date 'when free', the date when left, and 'observations'. From the register it can be seen that children were aged between five and fourteen and were sent by Overseers of the Poor from parishes all over England and the Governors of the Foundling Hospital. The only Cuckney child recorded was Peter Frogatt who was

Cuckney School in Nottinghamshire was a former mill and has sole fishing rights of the dam at its doorstep. The Headmaster is also the water bailiff

employed at the mill at the age of seven in 1792 and worked as an apprentice until he was twenty-one when he was deemed to be free.

The economics of employing children as opposed to apprenticing them and employing them 'when out of their times' were obviously clearly stated by the mill owners who were frustrated by the other mills who 'would certainly like them employ all the children therein that they could and must bring down the price of labour to the lowest ebb ...'

A benevolent picture of the jolly life of the apprentice is painted by Throsby in the History of Nottinghamshire:

Here are children from the foundling hospital, London, who are employed at the respective mills, and are kept in excellent order. They live in cottages, built for the purpose, under the care of superintendents; boys under one roof and girls under another: an apothecary attends them at stated times to preserve health. They are trained to the duties of religion and are fed plentifully. It is happy that these little aliens to kindred affection, should, by the bounty of the good and opulent, be made such useful members of society, and ornaments of philanthropy.

The 'ornaments of philanthropy' obviously did not share the view of the writer for the registers, though reticent on cause, speak eloquently on consequence: forty-seven died despite the apothecary's attendance 'to preserve health'; sixty ran away. Some children were transferred to other mills in the area but remained the responsibility of the Toplis firm.

4 August 1803

Sirs

Ann Harris ... arrived here on 25 July very ill and quite exhausted from want and fatigue upon the road ... Ann Harris was not bound originally to us nor did we receive any premium with her when we received her from Cuckney ... the Committee directed that you should be applied to, to reimburse the Hospital the expense it has incurred by your original agreement with this Committee as to Ann Harris ...

Others 'went for soldiers'. A great many did not run as far as the army, other mills or the long trek back to London – they could see little prospect of their young lives improving between the workhouse and the work at the mill, so ended it in the eight-acre dam.

Besides the '12 hours only' which the children worked there was compulsory church attendance and schooling in a schoolroom on site. The schoolmaster's house was alongside the apprentices' cottages. In 1832 a John Johnson was listed as schoolmaster and parish clerk. The mill ceased working in 1844. It was bought by the Duke of Portland who made it into the village school two years later for 200 children.

The Duchess of Portland was supporting a school at Norton Cuckney in 1832 for '35 poor girls', for whom she also provided frocks, cloaks and bonnets. The Duke transferred Cuckney School to the Vicar and Churchwardens by a trust deed in 1890, but it became beyond the financial means of the Church and became 'Controlled' in 1953 and funded by the County Education Committee. A separate Infant School was built in 1849, but closed in 1914 when the pupils were transferred to the mill to become an all-age school until the secondary school reorganisation in 1965.

The mill buildings were reduced by half and the top storey removed on its conversion to a school. As the local primary school it serves the villages of Cuckney, Holbeck, Nether Langwith, Norton and Welbeck and many lodges and farms in north-west Nottinghamshire and, on occasion, children from Derbyshire farmsteads and Church Warsop. They are encouraged to learn about the unique history of their school, which has a privilege probably unmatched anywhere else in the country, for by historical tenure the school has the sole fishing rights of the great lake and dam – and the headteacher is officially the water bailiff.

The village school started life in various ways up and down the country long before school buildings were built. While nothing has come to light in England and Wales comparable to the 'hedge schools' of Ireland, early lessons were carried out in whatever sheltered space was available at the time, many of the originals now lost without trace.

A letter dated 12 September 1736 mentions 'the Charity School of Albury', arguing the suitability of the schoolmaster for his post. A report from the Bishops Visitations of 1783 stated 'There is no public school, properly so called in this parish, only a small charity school, supported partly by voluntary subscriptions, partly by a settled endowment, the whole about £8 per annum, for 16 children'. This was mainly from accrued interest and rents from four thatched cottages in South Street in which the legacy was invested.

It would appear that Avebury village school was held for a hundred years in the parish church in a large wooden gallery, which stretched in the south aisle from the doorway to the west window at the back of the aisle. The gallery incorporated part of the medieval rood screen, salvaged at the Reformation when the Rood was ordered to be destroyed throughout the country. At great risk to themselves, the people of Avebury did not obey the decree of Elizabeth I to remove the rood loft, but concealed it behind a lath and plaster covering against the east wall of the nave; it was discovered during the Victorian restoration, and is one of the very few to survive.

The gallery school accommodated up to twenty children; the numbers, varying 'according to the season of the year'. The schoolmaster was appointed by the minister and churchwardens and was paid £10 a year in 1834 'a better schoolmaster could not be obtained at the present salary'.

SUBURBAN VILLAGES

As one who long in populous city pent,
Where houses thick and sewers annoy the air,
Forth issuing on a summer's morn to breathe
Among the pleasant villages and farms
Adjoin'd from each thing met conceives delight.

Milton, *Paradise Lost*

The definition of a village becomes more tenuous as one approaches the city, but many schools had their origins in villages which have since been swallowed up by a conurbation or urban sprawl. This has

Ham schoolchildren celebrating the coronation of George V in 1911. The school building is now a Roman Catholic Church

happened in the case of Richmond-upon-Thames – now part of Greater London – a borough which identifies four schools as originating from village schools.

Ham village school was affiliated to the National Society when a local committee was formed in 1817 to apply to the Earl of Dysart, the Lord of the Manor, for consent to a schoolroom being erected on ground adjoining the two almshouses on the Common. In the event a room was raised above the first floor of the almshouses (the poor house) for the purpose of a National School at the expense of the subscribers. A separate school for the Ham boys was provided in 1832 when a schoolroom, which doubled up as a vestry, was added to the eastern end of St Andrew's Church on the lower part of Ham Common; the infants were transferred to a building to the north of Cut-throat Alley, leaving the schoolroom above the almshouses to the girls. The boys' school served Ham and Hatch and the neighbouring parish of Petersham, there being no other boys' school at that time nearer than Kingston. The ornamental work required to ensure an architectural style in keeping with the church raised the cost to £400. Pupils paid 2d a week for their schooling, but two infants or more from the same family were admitted for 1½d each.

In the 1890s the parents' occupations reflected the rural community of Ham – gardener, carpenter, lock-keeper, carter, stoker, milkman, cowman, inn-keeper, dairyman, potato-dealer, shepherd, coachman, laundrywomen – when the population was a mere 1479, a figure which had increased six-fold by 1981. Children from the nearby National Orphan Home also attended the village school, the little orphan girls are identified in the turn of the century photographs by their close-cropped hair.

Despite rebuilding of the individual schools, all three schoolrooms became redundant in 1890 when new school buildings were completed to meet the requirements of the Education Department. The old St Andrew's School on the Common ceased to be an educational establishment in January 1966 and permission was granted for it to be a Roman Catholic Chapel of Ease. In January 1987 the old school was consecrated as the Church of St Thomas Aquinas.

A separate parish of St Richard's with its own modern church was created in 1966, and St Richard's with St Andrew's C. of E. Primary School was born on a modern housing estate.

The ties here are more than titular: spiritual and secular threads are woven into the very fabric of school life; the vicars of both churches regularly take school services, and as a Voluntary Aided School the Parochial Church Councils of St Andrew's and St Richard's – as well as Petersham parishes give financial support towards the upkeep of the school through an annual capitation fee to the Diocesan Board of Education.

Similarly, St Mary's and St Peter's School at Teddington is a Church of England School, subscribed to and represented by the parishes from whose churches it takes its twin name. Founded in 1832, four decades before education became compulsory, the villagers of Teddington appointed a committee to raise subscriptions for the building. HM Queen Adelaide, Consort of William IV, accompanied her royal approval to the establishment of a village school with a donation of £100 towards the initial costs – an interest she maintained by subscribing £5 a year until her death in 1849.

Teddington saw its most radical change from village to urban environment with the coming of the railway in 1863, when the old manor lands were sold for housing development. Despite enlargements, the increased population outgrew the old school and the Saints Peter and Paul Church now occupies the site. The school moved to a new building in 1974, taking the St Peter's part of that church's name to couple with St Mary's – of St Mary's with St Alban.

St Mary's of Twickenham has the same kind of background as

those just looked at in Ham and Teddington – with the exception of carrying but one church-linked name, and having the distinction of a foundation as early as 1645. Exceptionally, a girls' school was also in existence by 1648. The present school dates back to 1861 with later additions.

St Osmund's secluded in the semi-rural Thames-side village of Barnes, is a Voluntary Aided School, differing from the three already mentioned only insofar as its Christian principles are based on the Catholic religion, and having a very recent foundation. Founded in 1968, St Osmund's replaces the Convent Independent School.

Petersham, neighbouring Ham, owed its village school to Lord John Russell, the Prime Minister. Managed by the British and Foreign Bible Society, the little school stood in the ancient royal park of Richmond, just inside Petersham Gate and was bombed in 1943.

One might travel many miles and not find a more old-fashioned quaintly picturesque place than this little village – the river Cray, flowing through at the foot of the hamlet, adds to the beauty of the place and, with its large mill and millpond upon which are the inevitable ducks and geese, tenders completeness to the aspect.

Foots Cray, which included the one-time hamlet of Sidcup, could hardly be identified today from this description of less than a century ago. Godwin Foot's manor on the Cray, assessed at half a sulung at Domesday, has lost its identity to Sidcup and suburbia has swallowed up the agricultural industry which not so long ago kept pupils from their village school.

Benjamin Harenc founded the village school in 1815 and for the first year the children were taught in the church until the schoolhouse was built. Each child was required to pay one penny a week for the school fund from which rewards were distributed each quarter at the discretion of the Committee, comprised mainly by the Ministers and churchwardens of the parish and annual Subscribers of two guineas or more. The disbursements included rewards to the teachers as well as meritorious pupils. In 1815 the Master was paid £40 per annum, and the Mistress received £12.

To Edward Stevens, Susanna Ireman and John Peters, Teachers of the three classes, a pair of shoes, a cap and sixpence each. To John Francis, John Weeks and John Smith, assistants, a cap and sixpence each. Six children of each of the three classes received sixpence each. Every other child received one penny, and Mrs Trubman gave a dinner to the whole school.

1834 appears to have been a poor year in the school's annals: the children failed to show a proper respect for the authority of Master and Mistress so received no reward of clothing, the following year it was recorded that the Master had 'adopted a more conciliatory manner towards the children'.

The school was completely rebuilt in 1883 but closed in 1982. However, its old walls still resound to the happy sounds of boys at school. It is now an independent day prep school for boys registered as an educational charitable trust. The Victorian Jubilee clock tower stands proud against the skyline, testimony to the faith of the early founder, whose name Harenc School perpetuates by its traditional ethos.

SCHOOL BY DESIGN AND DEFINITION

I walk through the long school room questioning.

W. B. Yeats

School has been held in many different places in villages over the ages. The Neville-Grenvilles gave a late seventeenth-century cottage in the High Street to Butleigh to convert into a school about 1840.

At Dymock, school was held in the George – the pub next door – during alterations in 1884, and to accommodate the influx of evacuees from Birmingham in 1939, the local children moved to the Vicarage and the Parish Hall as the Shift System for Dymock children, from 8 a.m. to 12 noon, was seen to be unfair to them.

At Marshfield, Mrs Dionysia Long's School was a room above the Parish Lock-up; Ampney Crucis was left a barn by Sir Robert Pleydell as a Schoolroom; nearby, Meyseyhampton's School 'although possessing a painstaking and efficient master', had long been conducted in the kitchen of a tumble-down farmhouse. 'A bay of timber ready framed, lying in the barn to be adjoined to the house' was left by John Cooper for a schoolhouse at Long Marston, and the Duchess of Beaufort's School at Badminton formed the central feature of an almshouse block. At Westbury-on-Severn, school was held in a chantry chapel in the churchyard, and Minchinhampton housed its school in a small grange of Malmesbury Abbey and, at one time, in the wool marketing house.

Still in Gloucestershire, Oddington's most popular of its five small schools in 1835 was held at Manor Farm. At Naunton, school was housed in a room at the lovely Queen Anne Rectory until the National School was built in 1864 in the main street opposite the Baptist chapel, which had held its own British school from 1860. Close by the village green at Broadwell, school in 1833 was a cottage – grandly called the College.

Lord Wemyss was supporting a school at Church Stanway and its hamlet of Wood Stanway, where schoolteachers were recorded in the late eighteenth century. Two hundred years earlier Sherborne had a schoolmaster; the salary of £2 per year was claimed by the parish clerk in 1684. Smaller than the village of Sherborne in the Windrush Valley, was the market town of Stow-on-the-Wold on the Roman Fosse Way at the time when 'John Scolmarster' paid tax for his servant in 1381. Studham, settled in the shelter of Bedfordshire's Dunstable Downs, has its village school as one of four set up by the Ashridge Trust. Although scattered physically around its ancient common, the village is close-knit; the new school is neighbour to the old school.

Sited in quite different aspect, is East Ilsley School – exposed to the elements on top of a hill on Berkshire's rolling race-country downs. Beautiful and invigorating when the countryside is bathed in balmy summer, but barren and isolated in the grip of winter, the school has suffered in severe weather conditions when even the floors and first aid equipment have frozen. Getting to school has become something of a challenge since the Queen's racing stables village of West Ilsley lost its school in 1965, but the community spirit at East Ilsley is strong, and local people have seen to it that the children do not go hungry when, on occasion, the school dinners cannot get delivered. The village school here has, more than once, opened its doors in severe blizzard conditions to shelter and feed motorists stranded on the downs. On 13 December 1981, the log book records that during

Wookey Hole School was built by the mill for the children of their employees. The school stands to the right of the old paper-mill sheds

Windows on the World. A charity child and text scroll surmount a front window of Litton School

the evening over 400 people were given refuge, hot drinks and food, served by the school secretary and the chairman of the governors, in the village school high on the gallops scored downs.

Wookey Hole is a magical mystical place, locked in the lore and legend of its measureless caves and caverns with their deep green pools and soaring sparkling stalagmites. And above it all the old Domesday mill changed its purpose over the years to become a papermill by 1610 and was remodelled to take its place in the Victorian industrial age. The mill owners built houses, a church and a school for their employees to settle in the valley. The Log Book records: 'Wookey Hole weekday schools in the out Parish of S. Cuthbert, near Wells. Somerset, erected in 1871 by Messrs WS Hodgkinson & Co for the education of the children of those employed in their Paperworks, and of others resident in the immediate neighbourhood. Children were admitted on 8 April 1872 – 48 boys and 42 girls, most of whom had not been to school previously or had attended the local Dame School.'

Litton in Derbyshire had its school before it had a church. The present school, now a protected building, was built in 1868 on the initiative of Canon Samuel Andrew, with a parish library next door. Church was held in the school and when a church was built in the 1920s the old vestments and banners were left in a chest in the

Litton School on the edge of the village green where the old stocks supply amusement for today's schoolboys

Cheriton Fitzpaine School, Devon, is the longest thatched single building in Great Britain

school, together with Poor Law accounts and Apprentices schemes. Piecing together the fragments gleaned from the old records and local beliefs, it appears that the extraordinarily wide road through the village may once have been the bed of a stream supplying the local wool industry with fresh running water. Once the centre of a small lead mining trade, the school also served as an exchange point where unrefined lead ore was weighed and sold. Litton School has now reached a crucial stage in its own history when local people are fighting hard to keep their village school at the heart of their community.

Rhosgoch School of Painscastle near Builth Wells, built on traditional lines, replaces three old schools in other parishes. In a remote county area of Powys, drawing its pupils from the farm steads, the school calendar is still punctuated by real rural events such as the Ploughing Match, and is used by all the community groups in the evenings.

Cheriton Fitzpaine School must be one of the prettiest village schools in the kingdom. Unique in being Britain's longest thatched single purpose building, as opposed to a row of cottages or barns – its history is as long as its beautiful honey thatch roof. Abounding the churchyard, furnished with the lichen-encrusted tombstones of villagers who once lived and learnt and had their being within the thick cob stone walls of the old school, it already had a 'School Chamber' by 1648 in what was then the Long Room of the church, to which it adjoined. In 1754 the Church House part, which had long been an unregulated poorhouse, became the parish workhouse, with counting-house, workroom with spinning-wheels, dining-room, kitchen, pantry, brewhouse and storerooms, as well as the original school chamber.

By 1833 the village had two public day and three fee-paying schools, but by 1850 they came together as the parish school in the old school chamber, to become a Board School in 1876, when the present 'middle room' accommodated over 100 children.

Outstanding in the Devon hill village of many thatched buildings, the school butts above the village street, the upper storey of its whitewashed wall supported above the pavement by massive rustic pillars. The cobble path is thought to have been laid by French prisoners of war in the eighteenth century.

Among the Wiltshire thatch and flint and stone cottages, Great Wishford School, an attractive chequered brickwork building dating back to 1722, keeps close company with the parish church. The stone inscriptions on the churchyard wall must have afforded many a school-master with a ready arithmetic lesson, for here is recorded the price of bread: a difficult task to set today – decimal conversion apart – for it is given in price per gallon, recalling the days when it was sold by volume.

Brick buildings were fairly uncommon in medieval Oxfordshire until the Earl of Suffolk moved to Ewelme on his marriage to Alice Chaucer. Alice, the granddaughter of the great poet Geoffrey Chaucer, and her Earl built the Church of St Mary on the top terrace of the Chilterns as they fold around this historic village. They also built the almshouses below and a grammar school in 1437 on the lower ledge. The school has served the village for over five-and-a-half centuries, now as a Primary School. Village children still gaze up at the original beam roof structure in the top storey classroom, just as they did in Chaucer's day, just as they did when Henry VIII was honey-mooning at the manor house, and just as they did when they heard of the first man walking on the moon. School has never been anywhere else but here; built for its purpose, Ewelme School is unique now by being the oldest village school in the country in its original building.

Avebury had its School in 1844, under the authority of the School Sites Act and became known successively as 'the National', 'Parochial', C of E, then 'Primary', with complex conveyances regarding the site on which it stands – given as 33 feet 9 inches by 18 feet; 1,743 square feet; and 'a measurement of 12 poles or thereabouts' on three different deed polls.

The old school at Widecombe in the Moor is next door to the church

Avebury village is a Conservation Area within the ancient stone circle, and the proximity to the curious stones created considerable difficulties when the school needed to be enlarged and modernised. To conform with the regulations regarding ancient monuments, a new school building had to be built behind the old school and now serves also the villages of Beckhampton, West Kennett, Winterbourne Monkton and Berwick Bassett.

The church, being the only public building in the village in the days before village halls were thought of, was used as a school in many other villages. At Surrey's Long Melford, which has one of the longest village streets in the country, a multiplication table on the east wall of the Lady Chapel is still to be seen today, 200 years after the chapel in the ornately flint-decorated Church of the Holy Trinity served the village as a schoolroom.

Widecombe held its first school in the granite church house which was built at the same time as the early sixteenth-century church tower. Facing the village square and close by the entrance to the church, the church house performed the function of a hostel for churchgoers who travelled many miles to the pretty Devon village in the moorland valley. The house was used as other similar church house inns and a lease of 1608 stipulated that it was 'on condition that parishioners were allowed to keep ale once or twice a year and to use the said house as they have been accustomed'. After serving for a time as an almshouse, it became the village charity school and as the Board school from 1878 until 1932 when a new school was built at the bottom of the hill beyond the old smithy. It now belongs to the National Trust.

Gorsley Goff is the only school in the country still perpetuating the name of Edward Goff, a self-educated Herefordshire farm labourer, who became a very prosperous coal merchant. Walking to London to seek employment as a clerk was Edward Goff's first steps into the business world. He died in 1813 a devout Baptist and wealthy philanthropist, leaving money to promote or establish some thirty schools in his home and neighbouring counties.

Baptists at nearby Ryeford held their services at the blacksmith's shop and in a house called Blindman's Gate, they then looked to Gorsley as a station for preaching the Gospel. The trustees of Goff's Charity built Gorsley Goff's School as a Chapel-cum-School in 1821, the pastor being the schoolmaster. Under the influence of successive worthy pastors both religion and education flourished; a new Baptist Chapel was built in 1852 leaving the early Chapel to become the village school under masters with strong Non-conformist ties, either as pastor, deacon or lay preacher.

Despite the non-denominational teaching clause practised at Gorsley Goff's, the Anglicans built their own Church of England School as a Church-cum-School on the brow of the hill. The church – in identical architectural style – shares the hill.

Two schools in the same village caused no little confusion. Gorsley C. of E. was at the top of the hill, but Gorsley Goff at the bottom was strictly in the parish of Linton – and Linton had its own C. of E. village school, so the Education Authority, in the way they are wont, decided that it should be called Linton/Gorsley Goff's School.

Gorsley C. of E. School lasted only a few years. Registers exist from 1886 to 1907 and record payments of School pence.

The rivalry between Church and Chapel extended to Linton village, a feud which has now passed into local folklore as Gorsley Goff survived and became remodelled to take its place in the modern world.

The village school at Summerseat in Lancashire is a Methodist/Wesleyan foundation of 1842. Ribchester closed its Roman Catholic School in 1985 and the pupils transferred quite happily to the Church of England School. It was a schoolboy who found the ceremonial helmet some 200 years ago, belonging to the Roman fort which lies below this terraced street village in the Ribble Valley.

Victorian schools often reflect their ecclesiastical connections in their design. Little Gaddesden School, founded by Lord Brownlow of Ashridge and church aided, with its carved windows and shaped gutters, is often mistaken for the church.

Similarly mistaken for the church is the school at Great Tew, the

Great Tew, picturesquely set on the village green bordered with thatched cottages, the pub and shop

epitome of an English village idyll. Secluded from the main traffic arteries of Oxfordshire, Great Tew is found only by those who seek – down winding tree-shaded lanes where gypsies camp in beech-hung clearings. The Cotswold stone-built school stands on a rise flanking one side of a triangular village green encircled by tall trees, their shifting shadows dancing across the squares of the hopscotch patch in the playground. Thatched cottages, all in a row – rose-clad and creeper-clung – with village shop and pub among them, complete what must be one of the prettiest country corners in the kingdom.

Closer to the industrial conurbations of what is known as the West Midlands, is Netherton. Its church connections can truly be said to be closer than most for it is thought that Netherton came by its first school from what might be classed as the change from building the church! St Andrew's Church was consecrated in 1830 – a 'Waterloo Church', built with funds given by the Ecclesiastical Commissioners by the House of Commons for the building of churches 'as a thanks offering to Almighty God for the country's deliverance from the tyranny of Napoleon'. The money left over was used for building a school on land given, or sold, by the Badley family of Pear Tree Lane to the Blue Coat Trustees of Dudley in 1836 'for the education of poor boys and girls resident in the neighbourhood according to the principles and doctrine of the Church of England'.

The Kingswinford, Brettell Lane Board School in Staffordshire began its educational life in 1882 in the (Wesleyan) Methodist Chapel. The school had to be given half-holidays when the chapel trustees used it, and charged the school £1 per annum for use of the harmonium.

At Powerstock, school used to be held in a medieval church nave which nearly bankrupted its founder. The village, set among the deep lanes of Dorset below the ramparts of Eggardon Hill, is the seat of many ancient customs.

An old eighteenth-century barn became Aynho School; first recorded when accepted into the National Society in 1813. An infant classroom was added in 1896, and a toilet block in 1973, but the Northamptonshire school closed in 1985 with only twelve pupils on roll.

Gartheli School in the remote and beautiful Welsh heartland, started at 'Athen' in 1871. Built on the River Meurig, it suffered from extensive flooding and a new school was built in 1913 on an acre of land given by Daniel and Sarah Jones and Hendre Philip. One of the last of the traditional school buildings, with characteristic bell-dome, to be built this century, the school has recently suffered notice of closure and its future determined by politics and finance.

Infant classroom showing gallery at Finstock School in 1904

Cheddon Fitzpaine's School originated in 1793 in cottages on the same site as the Victorian building now stands. Fourth and fifth generations of the same Somerset families are now attending the old village school.

Promoters of schools in England and Wales were required to submit plans to the Committee of Council on Education to be approved and sealed by Their Lordships. The detailed plans had to be on tracing calico.

Among the twenty-nine rules, specific heights to ceiling or collar beams were calculated according to area of floor space. If built of brick, the external walls were to be at least one brick and a half in thickness; if of stone, at least 20 inches in thickness.

Other specifications stated.

The doors and fireplaces in schoolrooms for children above 7 years of age must be so placed as to allow of the whole of one side of the schoolroom being left free for the groups of benches and desks.

There must be no opening wider than an ordinary doorway between an infants' and any other schoolroom, as it is necessary to stop the sound of the infant-teaching.

An infant school should always be on the ground floor and, if exceeding 80 children in number, should have two galleries of unequal size, and a small group of benches and desks for the occasional use of the elder infants. No infant Gallery should hold more than 80 or 90 infants.

The classrooms should be fitted up with a gallery placed at right angles with the window.

Framed wood partitions are not allowed between schoolrooms and classrooms. They must be separated by lath and plaster partition, or a wall.

The windows should be of glass set in wood or iron casements. Lead lights and diamond panes are not allowed.

The sills of the windows should be placed not less than 4 feet above the floor.

The residence for the Master or Mistress, containing a parlour, a kitchen, a scullery and three bedrooms – each of the bedrooms to have a fireplace – was to similar specifications; there to be no internal communication between the residence and the school, with a separate porch, and no iron or wooden building approved.

Playgrounds had to be separate for boys and girls.

The privies were the subject of close attention: apart from them being separate for the two sexes they had to be sub-divided with a door and light to each, and the children were not to pass in front of the residence on their way to their offices.

Uniformity of furnishings as well as architectural style are the quintessence of the village school. Today the walls sing with colour; alive with texture of the children's own artwork – their interpretation of their experience. The sepia prints and subdued shades of the scriptural scenes, inspired by patriotism and aimed at moralising by visual impact, have been regaled to the once-upon-a-time. But who could look again at *The Boyhood of Raleigh, When Did you last see your Father?*, or *The Light of the World* and not recall a school classroom?

UNIFORM AND IDENTITY

School uniform originated in the charity schools where distinctive clothing for pupils formed part of the benefaction. Many of the schools became known by the colour of the pupils' coats, hence the Red Boys' School of Stroud, founded in 1642 by a local clothier for 'two honest poor widows to breed up four poor children' in the schoolroom below a wool loft in the Market House, and the Cirencester Blue School, founded in 1714, which educated 100 children for half days only so that the rest of the day could be spent in 'profitable labour for their parents at home'. Even so, the pupils wrote their way through some 8,200 quills in the first ten years, at a cost of £2 4s. In addition to their clothing the pupils received free hair cuts, for which an Aaron Sparrow had the contract for two shillings a year.

The Blue Coat Schools appear frequently south of the Midlands. Bredon Hancocks School, set in a tree-shaded village street, neighbour to the thatched and half-timbered Fox and Hounds, originated as a Blue Coat Boys School. Since its foundation in 1718 by William Hancock when it was 'all-age' the Vale village school has changed role from Secondary Modern to Primary, and is now a First

Bredon Blue Coat School neighbours the thatched village pub

School. In the Cotswold village of Bisley, the Blue Coat School was left in 1732 in charge of the founder's clothier friends, but, having failed to provide trusteeship after their death, the school suffered a period when no rent charge was collected for the charity. The foundation was to teach 10 poor boys in Bisley to read and write and to clothe them. In 1829 the master was receiving a salary of 12 guineas a year, and the clothing cost £18 6s. 6d. Wotton-under-Edge had its Blue Coat School from an endowment of 1630.

The distinctive Blue Coat uniform girls in blue gowns and round caps and white aprons; the boys in blue coats and waistcoats with white collar-tabs – survive today mainly in statues; in the famous Blue Coat School at Harborne, now a public school and in niches high up in old school walls. In the parish church at Cirencester there is a very detailed painted figure of an eighteenth-century Bluecoat Boy, hat in one hand, a book in the other, which used to stand in the magnificent south porch to beg funds for the charity schools. Uniforms for the village school are still partly funded from a trust formed from an ancient charity described on a benefaction board in the church at Feckenham. 'King Charles the First of Blessed Memory Gave to ye ffree scoole of ffeckenham y yearly Sume of £6 thirteen shillings and ffoure Pence Payable out of ye fforest land'.

From all benefactions of their respective villages, Stelling Minnis schoolboys were allowed grey coats with green capes, to be worn at

Sitting among her pupils, the Headmistress listens in to story-time at Ampney Crucis in the 1980s

divine service twice a day, each Easter. Fur tippets for the girls, smock frocks and leathern breeches for the boys were provided by Madame Rucker for the pupils of her school, built in the garden of Bowden Hall at Upton St Leonards, across the fields from Prinknash Abbey.

The bequest of Robert Pleydell, who endowed the village school at Ampney Crucis in the Cotswolds in 1722, included clothing for its poor pupils. The boys were provided with white linen shirts, blue coats, waistcoats and caps, leather breeches, black leather shoes and blue worsted stockings (to be knitted by the girls). The girls had the same kind of shoes and stockings; white calico frocks, petticoats and whalebone stays, blue capes and black beribboned straw bonnets. If the local dressmaker could not make the clothes, the headmistress was obliged to do so!

The orphan girls of Cheltenham's School of Industry made their own clothes as part of their lessons in needlework. Their uniform comprised brown serge gowns, straw bonnets or caps, black worsted stockings and mittens, white tippets, check bibs and aprons, and a duffield cloak'. Each girl also wore a medallion round her neck bearing the name of the institution and her registration number.

In the spring of 1920 I began school. There was precious little imagination about the manner in which children were dressed for school. An ancient school photograph displays an interesting variety of individuality ranging from Sailor type tunics to starched collars worn outside a jacket or jersey, while several boys wore puttees probably brought home by their dads on demobilisation. The girls were probably a little more uniform in appearance since so many of them wore white pinafores and button-up boots.

Phil Bridgman, Cott Abbey, Glos.

Today, the majority of village primary schools have a school uniform – worn with the pride of belonging to an identifiable group akin to the knights of old showing their king's colours.

Colsterworth village school remembers Sir Isaac Newton, who was born on Christmas Day 1642 at the local Woolsthorpe Manor, by incorporating the synonymous apple as the letter 'O' in the school name. The apple logo was introduced fairly recently and is used on pupils' sweatshirts as well as the official school paper. The old National School building which served this large Lincolnshire village for a hundred years until the new school was built, is next to the church, inside which there is a sundial cut by the great scientist when he was but a schoolboy of nine years old.

The medieval castle, whose impressive jagged ruins are the dominant feature of Sheriff Hutton, is translated into the school badge. The school has privileged access to what remains of the castle, the favoured Yorkshire residence of Richard III.

Hemington School adopted the hornbeam tree as their emblem,

Willingly to school in the 1980s. Note the old school sign

since researching their history had begun with calculating the age of the tree – which was reckoned to be in the field before the school was built in 1877. The green of the tree against the blue of the sky was also a symbolic choice for the school colours.

The advent of the motor introduced a new visual sign of the times: 'Warning notices to Motorists' were introduced outside Gloucestershire schools in 1910. The signs, too, have changed with the times: from the beacon to the schoolchildren with their satchels, to today's featureless outlines of a boy and girl.

3 *People of the Schools*

MASTERING SCHOOL

This reminds one of the parish where a stupid old man was set to be a schoolmaster, because he was past keeping the pigs.

Florence Nightingale, *Notes on Nursing*

Contemporaneous with Florence Nightingale's drive to attract more educated women to the nursing profession, was that of the establishment of a Committee of the Privy Council to superintend the application of any sums voted by Parliament for the purpose of promoting public education. This necessitated the institution of HM Inspectorate and it is from the official inspections of schools that we are given the first comprehensive assessment of the curriculum and the quality of those 'set to teach school'.

The lowly status and lack of professional skill of the teachers were tied to lack of adequate funds for maintaining the buildings, meagre budgets for resources and poor pay. These inter-related causes and consequences were particularly noticeable in the village schools and the first inspections in 1844 of the Western District – extending from Warwickshire to Cornwall – bore out Florence Nightingale's caustic example.

It was a shepherd who 'being too infirm at 80 to look after the sheep' undertook the education of the children at Winstone School, but he did teach 'very elementary writing' – an advance on the parish clerk's efforts at neighbouring Duntisborne Abbots for it was deemed he had 'no skill for teaching', and the mistress at Badgeworth was said to be 'almost as strikingly ignorant as the children'. An illiterate labourer who had been 'forced to give up his work by old age and crippled by rheumatism' was master at Stoke Orchard; and a yeoman who had 'fallen upon evil days – untrained, inefficient, with no control over the children' was in charge of Thornbury School, which had no books, no slate pencils and no maps.

The Revd H. W. Bellairs, HMI, an Oxford graduate, who undertook the inspection found that the teacher was generally regarded as no more than 'a kind of necessary appendage'. Such was the regard for the low status of the teacher from the early nineteenth century that a Forest of Dean woman wrote the letter of application on behalf of her husband in 1815 for the mastership of Bisley Blue Coat School. She was at great pains to explain why such a respectable man 'has been necessitated to teach school, the only resource for honest poverty that has not been brought up either to trade or labour'.

Such revelations bear out the dicta expressed by Florence Nightingale 'a general disgust or incapacity for other things'; George Bernard Shaw 'those that can, do, those that can't, teach ...'; and the educationalist the Revd Francis Close 'the commonest qualification for school teaching was failure at one's trade, especially shoemaking or tailoring'.

Hardwicke Reformatory, where John Prichard, Beatrix Potter's 'Tailor of Gloucester', was schoolmaster, was one of the most influential of the special schools set up to reclaim children from the life of crime which Charles Dickens so graphically portrayed in his works. The Reformatory was founded in 1852 in buildings on Hardwicke estate by T. B. Lloyd Baker; the curriculum was divided between formal lessons, religious training and physical work on the heavy clay of the Severnside farmland attached to the school. Two years after its opening, the Hardwicke experiment was praised in a leading article in *The Times* and even after its closure in 1922 has been widely imitated, its principle forming the basis of contemporary methods of treating the young offender.

Punishments were ordinarily by a system of fines, 'a light use of the cane' or by a short period of solitary confinement upon bread and water in a light cell. Compared with many schools' board, the fare was nourishing and wholesome with 'occasionally half a pint of common cider and a little tea and butter on Sundays'.

John Prichard moved to Charlton Kings and died of pulmonary tuberculosis at the age of fifty-seven in 1934. He is buried in the cemetery and on the kerbstone of his grave is engraved the legend 'The Tailor of Gloucester'.

The village schoolmaster proper of Charlton Kings was 'Boss' Fry, remembered by the pupils of the locally known 'Crab End College' for his total commitment to education in its broadest sense. He was a native of the village, his family and roots were there – he understood the pattern of village life. He also knew and respected the magnetic draw of the town for the country boy, therefore he introduced them to the beauty and interests of their Cotswold hillsides seeking to impress upon them the joy of the field and wold rather than the temptations of town streets and alleys. In the same way, he built up a school library.

No Bodleian, in fact just three closely packed rows of books in the top of an old cupboard, but we found it full of magic. He would draw a class round

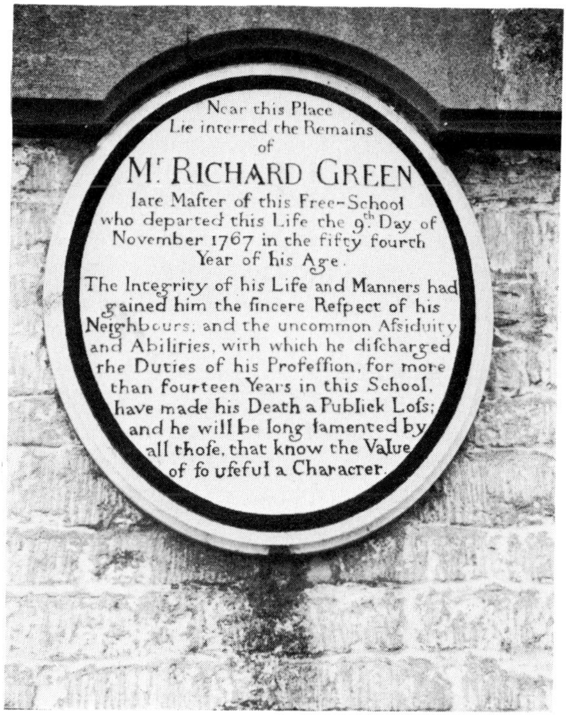

The village schoolmaster – 'so useful a character'

him, perch upon his high stool, and producing some fascinating story, commence to read. Part way through, when there was no doubt that the story had gripped, the book was quietly closed. 'Well, there it is,' said he, 'if you liked it, it is in the library. You can finish it for yourselves.'

George Ryland, former pupil and later teacher of Charlton Kings Boys School, Glos.

Schoolmasters' sons often followed in the footsteps of their schoolmaster fathers. When John Roseblade retired as master of Barnes National Schools on the Green, the Lords of the Manor presented him with land on the Common on which to build a house to live in. The records did not say whether James, his son who succeeded him as schoolmaster and rate-collector, was as irascible as the old man – who caned the boys in church if they misbehaved.

Years of matching discipline with the wiles of village youth, the greater need for personal comforts, with less time to attend to their domestic matters and the initial awe of authority diminished by long acquaintance, bred many characters among the village schoolmasters and mistresses.

Great Dodfordians used to chant:

Grummy Jelfs is a very good man,
He tries to learn us all he can –

of Mr Jelfs, who reigned supreme in his little kingdom from 1884 until 1916. He is remembered for his strict discipline, falling asleep in the woods while the pupils rambled around on a nature walk and finally home, catching his pony, taking his ducks to the pond and salting his bacon, his salty language during erratic science lessons and his straw hat.

Hugh Hughes, the longest serving Head of Borthygest School, appeared to have been keen on allowing the children to witness the weddings and funerals of his native Welsh village. When the master's goat died at Withington 'Pop' Curtis remembered the schoolchildren had to follow behind the handcart to attend its burial in the nearby playing-field.

Early foundations would appear to have been far more selective in their appointment of schoolmaster than the desperate times in which state education was fostered. However, references to masters being 'licensed to teach' allude to the oath of allegiance to the supremacy of the Established Church – a political rather than an academic qualification. Many posts of a similar public nature required a licence from the bishop of the diocese and such a licence, enacted by the Act of Uniformity of 1662 and the Test Act of 1673, was couched in the following terms:

> This is to certify that ———— Schoolmaster of ———— hath now before me, the day and year aforesaid, solemnly taken the oath of allegiance and supremacy according to the form of words in that case provided and appointed. In witness thereof I have here unto subscribed my hand the day and year above.
>
> Signed ————
> Surrogate

The exclusion of Roman Catholics and Nonconformists from holding public office, as a result of the Act making a condition of appointment that all should subscribe to the form of Sacrament practised in the Church of England, led to bitter opposition. The Act of Toleration of 1689 went some way in lessening the stranglehold of the Church on Dissenters, but sectarian discrimination was an issue over which the Whigs and Tories battled until Lord John Russell's bill of 1828. As the majority of the founders were from the landed gentry supporting the Tories, many indentures specify the precise religious qualification of the schoolmaster.

Schoolmistresses were always paid less than their male counterparts and were subjected to stricter rules. Susannah Crump of Minsterworth left £4 a year for 'a discreet schoolmistress'. If a lady teacher married she automatically forfeited her employment.

Miss Kate Williams married in 1896 she then had to relinquish her post.
Ysgol Morfa Bychan, Gwynedd

M. D. Graves MCP, the master chosen to run the Chartist village school at Heronsgate in Hertfordshire in 1848, obviously sought to better the status of both his estate school and himself – pretentiously calling the school O'Connorville College to attract boarders from the families of grocers and cheesemongers rather than the poor allottees – and gaining a prize from Queen Adelaide and a letter from Queen Victoria for his pen-and-ink sketches.

Despite the regulations forbidding personal observations, school Log Books are filled with innuendoes directed at the parents, the Board, the Vicar, My Lords and any body impeding the Heads'

Britain's most durable teacher. David Rhys Davies, head of Dame Anna Child's Endowed School

intention of raising the standard of their schools. Noticeable among the mainly guarded remarks are those directed at the Heads' predecessors, occasionally the comments are downright forthright.

2 April 1872 — I undertook the Mastership of the above school March 25, as a permanency. The late Master, of whom I know nothing, must certainly have adopted a very peculiar method in teaching.

Viney Hill National School, Glos.

It were better to perish
than to continue schoolmastering …

Thomas Carlyle

Contrary to Carlyle's reckoning, 'schoolmastering' became more a way of life than a means of a living. School histories are punctuated with long-serving masters and mistresses, but modern-day legislation now imposes its own limits on longevity – so the record for being the 'most durable teacher' can never be broken.

David Rhys Davies, Headmaster of Dame Anna Child's Endowed School at Whitton in Powys, was still working in 1928 at the age of 92, and earned a place in the Guinness Book of Records. David Davies started his career as a pupil teacher, then teacher before becoming Headmaster – a total teaching service of 76 years and 2 months.

PEOPLE OF THE SCHOOLS

In quibbles, angel and archangel join,
And God the Father turns a school divine.

Alexander Pope, *On Paradise Lost*

Kempsford, the ancient seat of the earls of Lancaster on the Upper Thames, had a schoolmaster as early as 1693 to whom Lord Weymouth paid £5 a year. By 1735 a charity school was teaching poor children to read free of charge, for 2d a week they could learn to write; wealthier families were charged 1d for reading and 4d for writing. The founder laid down strict rules for the school: the master was to be 'of sober and religious conversation' and attend Divine Service 'at all times appointed' to set an example to the children in his care for whom he was also responsible for their cleanliness, neatness and decent dress for church service. School hours were from 6 a.m. to 6 p.m. from Lady Day to Michaelmas, and 'as near these hours as daylight will permit' for the best part of the year.

In the Cotswold village of Great Barrington the Headteacher

during the First World War was also the postmaster. Mr Barrett kept his pupils up-to-date with such news as he was privileged to receive first, and as the majority of families could not afford a daily paper parents would anxiously await their children's return from school to catch up on the war news.

Besides the lords and ladies of the manor and the local vicar who considered it their bounden duty to take a practical and moral interest in the village school, most villages had benevolent friends who gave a great deal of support in the early difficult years. Abinger Hammer had such a friend in Miss Laura Forster. It was Miss Forster who gave the occasional mental arithmetic and geography lesson and 'heard the infants sing'; when an inspection showed the Lower School to be 'not altogether satisfactory as to the sewing' (which would affect the grant) she provided the materials, took the lessons and undertook to sell the things made. It was Miss Forster who subscribed £5 – the extra cost of a Mistress in 1890; and her nephew, the novelist E. M. Forster, who was instrumental in arranging for the adoption of the school during the Second World War by Hamilton College in Upper New York State.

19 Oct 1944 The school connected to the main electric supply paid for by Miss Howson, Llys Cyngar to remember her friend Miss Townshend. Miss Howson always gave

Sports Day at Kempsford

vegetables, eggs and cocoa to the school kitchen and presented a piano to the school on an indefinite loan.

Ysgol Morfa Bychan, Gwynedd

It was the squire Sykes who made Sledmere the picture book village of the East Riding Wolds. Described as Yorkshire's own Sir Roger de Coverley, Sir Tatton Sykes continued the work of his father and turned the rough and barren countryside into well-cultivated estate farmland. The attractive school, once part of the church, was described by Sir John Betjeman as 'deliciously pseudo'.

On a North Yorkshire hillside above Kilburn the White Horse is a remnant of a project carried out by the village school of Husthwaite in 1857 when, under the direction of the local schoolmaster, the pupils marked the 314 foot long outline for some thirty local men to dig out.

Time sets a strange value on yesterday's misdemeanours and today's graffiti may well hold tomorrow's tourist attraction, for the 'I woz 'ere' inked on a school loo door may be the very stuff that future historians will preserve – if the author of the statement rises to fame or fortune. For most schoolchildren cutting their name into a desk would be cause for punishment, but having done just that – the desk that William Wordsworth carved into has been preserved for the 200 years since he left the village school at Hawkshead for Cambridge – so may well he might write when famous:

A Poet! He hath put his heart to school.

Sports shields at Sledmere in the Yorkshire Wolds

The grammar school was founded in 1585 by the Archbishop of York. In Wordsworth's time about 100 boys were taught classics and mathematics. A quotation from his *Personal Talk* is painted around the walls of the schoolroom above the diamond-pane windows.

Generations of children made their mark, literally but anonymously, at Coleshill School at Amersham by sharpening their slate pencils on the brick walls of the school – the marks are still to be seen.

John Constable loved 'every stile and stump, and every lane in the village' of his Suffolk birthplace. But his father, the wealthy miller of Flatford Mill – the subject of one of Constable's most famous paintings – did not choose the local village school for his son's education, sending him to Dedham, the next village along the Stour. The grammar school which he attended is now private houses, marked with an inscription that Thomas Grimwood was master in 1732.

East Bergholt has had a village school since 1594, the Lambe School is still intact, and the present Primary School in School Lane is the third building. As host to the East Bergholt Music School, involving over a hundred children, the village retains an arts connection albeit in different vein. St Mary's Church, which has its bells outside in the churchyard and a stained-glass memorial window to Constable, there is an enigmatic inscription to John Mattison, who died in 1723: 'eleven years the beloved Schoolteacher of this Town, then unfortunately Shott' – by whom or why he was shot, it does not say.

Another Suffolk village of great character is Lavenham. Its history was built on the East Anglian wool trade and the buildings of the old merchants stand sentinel to its past prosperity and the villagers' present regard for preservation. It was at Lavenham in her home village, that Jane Taylor wrote the well-known nursery rhyme, 'Twinkle, twinkle, Little Star'.

Nursery rhymes at Mells have deeply significant connotations. It was Jack Horner of Mells, the Abbot of Glastonbury's steward, who was sent with a gift of a large Christmas pie to Henry VIII in the hope that the King would be bribed into saving Glastonbury Abbey from dissolution. Little Jack Horner rested on his long journey to London, 'sat in a corner', looked wonderingly at the special pie 'stuck in his thumb and pulled out a plum' ... the 'plum' being the deeds of the Manor of Mells – and, claimed the deeds himself. The Horners have been Lords of the Manor of Mells ever since. The rhyme is said to have appeared in 1725.

Mells School is just outside the village. Originating as one of the oldest schools in the West Country, founded by the Lord of the Manor, the present school was originally the girls' school; the boys

Once a master weaver's house, Mells School corners the village green in Little Jack Horner's country

had their school by the church. Edging one of the village's several greens, the school was once an old master weaver's house. The weaving sheds have been converted and with an additional wing the school accommodates both Infants and Primary children.

Dick Whittington is more than a folk figure; the Mercers of London have given funds for the restoration of the church which stands on its own hill with Pauntley Court where Richard Whittington was born, and the Poet Laureate, John Masefield, promoted a fund for the rambling old house to become a Home for Young Wayfarers – offering to read his poems at any place within forty miles of his home if £25 was paid to the fund.

The story of Selborne is quite a different classic. The Revd Gilbert White, the eighteenth-century naturalist, immortalized the little Hampshire village through his brilliant observations of its antiquities, natural history and wildlife. It was Gilbert White, the author's grandfather, who left money in 1735 'to teach poor children in Selborne to read and write, say their prayers and catechism, to sew and to knit'; the foundation for the present village school. According to the Select Committee's report on the education of the poor, the White School was still in operation in 1818, albeit with but 10 pupils.

Plestor House and The Wakes, Gilbert White's house which dates back to 1500, now a museum, were reckoned as the only two

The long disused C. of E. School at Gorsley, which was once used for church services, overshadows its close neighbour the parish church. The consecrated east end of the old school, with its dominant window, was curtained off during school-time

substantial houses in the poor parish in 1840 when an appeal was launched for a new school building. In 1844 Bush Down Church of England School was opened, typical of the village school style of that date. Its early years were also typical of the rural school: hop-picking season governed the date for the summer holiday, and inducements made by way of money prizes for attendance. Attainment was also rewarded – appropriately, Charles Hoare for best performance in Standard IV in 1884 received Gilbert White's *Selborne*.

The abundance of golden gorse, from which Gorsley got its name, studded the wasteland between the dense woods of this Herefordshire border village to the advantage of yesterday's vagabonds and wayfarers. Some families even explored the village school.

I remember two gypsy children coming to the Gorsley Church School, they were always late for school. The boy would creep in and sit in the knee-hole of Mrs Crossland's desk and pull faces at us when her back was turned. The mother would come to see them at dinner-time, bringing them cake which she hid in her bosom.

Venice Watkins, Gorsley, Herefords.

The village school at Gorsley involved the whole family:

Dad took the boys for cricket in the summer and football in the winter, and we held the summer parties at our home at Brook Farm, opposite the Sugar Tump – the village green. After tea at the trestle tables under the cherry trees, we had races and games in the field. Children brought a poor dinner to school in those days, mostly bread and lard, but they would sit in front of the old tortoise stove toasting their sandwiches. Our family sat by the open fire. One day teacher's lunch-time cutlery was missing. She appealed for its return. Two days later a gipsy family, who lived in a real Romany caravan, brought her a big bunch of wild flowers, inside them was the cutlery wrapped in newspaper. My mother thanked them for the flowers and said no more.

Mrs Evelyn Young

I started my education at the village school at the age of 3 and retired from the Headship of it at the age of 65. When I was a child our Head took a great interest in our behaviour out of school as well. Discipline was exceptional. I benefited greatly from those early lessons. The Three R's were the most important, and we had Algebra to Quadratic Equations and learnt Latin roots. We had Dictation daily from the Editor's article in the Nottingham Guardian, hence most scholars were good spellers!

A good percentage always passed for Higher Education and qualified for good positions. I gained a Scholarship at 12.

Mrs E. Goodacre, Notts.

Returning to her old village school as Headmistress, where she had started as a child of three-and-a-half, was Winifred Brooks, remembered in Felmersham as one of the old-style teachers dedicated to her vocation, instituting annual May Day revels and keeping a photographic record of schooldays spanning half a century. The newly built school, too, follows the tradition of the old National for it is still the hub of village activity being designed from the beginning as a school-cum-community centre.

PUNISHMENTS

There is now less flogging in our great schools than formerly, but then less is learned there; so what the boys get at one end they lose at the other.

Samuel Johnson

It was to Appleby Magna in Leicestershire that the great Dr Johnson made his way in 1738, shortly after he had left his home town for London. Although he had been a schoolmaster, as well as a bookseller, in Lichfield for some six years, he failed to obtain the headmastership he sought at the Sir John Moore village school. It is said that influential friends had failed to obtain for him a degree of

Punishment book and cane

Trinity College, Dublin. The school's most notable pupil was the statesman, William Huskisson, whose death in 1830 was the result of the first railway accident.

Every School must have a Punishment Book in which all cases of corporal punishment must be recorded.

Administrative Memorandum No. 51

...and so the pages of the statutory punishment book bear witness to the sins of yesterday's miscreants. Many a small and wondering eye must have looked balefully up to the brightly coloured scriptural picture *Suffer Little Children* as the whiplash of a swishy cane hit through thin trouser seats, across the calves of bare-legged girls or tingled tender hands. The rod was not spared for the fairer sex: an entry for 1930 records eight strokes on a disobedient Betty; and an Elizabeth, who purloined a stick of chalk from the Infants' Room received six of the best; leap-frogging in the playground earned an erstwhile Edith four strokes.

Barry Round was seen smoking a pipe in the school yard. I took it from him and cautioned the boys about smoking.

Netherton, Worcs., 1867

Have had suspicion that some of the boys used tobacco, and today obtained full proof of the same. For this fault administered corporal punishment to Thomas, Fred and Robert Roe, also to Herbert Hunt and Thomas Noble.

Besthorpe, Notts., Dec. 1883

The boys were full of impudence and cheek and Mr John Horsey, Mr William Tilly and both the Daniel Tillys all kept a bundle of birch rods in a jar of water, to keep them supple. This and a strong right arm helped them to maintain order.

Lovington, Som.

An alternative punishment to the cane, birch or swish – used with injurious abandon even by the monitors in some schools – was a placard advertising the misdemeanour hung around the offender's neck. Complaints about the liberal use of corporal punishment inspired the idea of the dunce's cap. The humiliation of wearing the dunce's cap was often harder to bear than the physical pain.

7 May 1873 Mrs Drew called and complained that her girl had been beaten so severely that the flesh was cut upon her hand: she stated also that she had shown it to a respectable woman as a proof it was true. I sent for the child, who came, but the mother was unable to show even a mark on her girl, an example of how too many mothers in the Forest teach their children almost from infancy to lie and deceive.

Viney Hill National School, Glos.

A delicious picture is conjured up of how a Mrs Baxter dealt with miscreants of Eastleach in the 1850s. School was held in a room near the river alongside which the poet-curate John Keble walked between the two churches of Turville and Martin. Mrs Baxter 'always wore a small black bonnet frilled with Valenciennes lace. Over a tightly-bodiced and extremely full skirt she always wore a lilac, besprigged apron – to which disobedient children were pinned'.

Mr James Sheppard, Headmaster for the first thirty-seven years at Abinger Hammer, had his famous trio, three sticks which were placed by the oil lamps to try. Culprits then chose a stick by name before receiving punishment. The names varied slightly through the years – Hardington Park, Hemington School, Burnt Cork, Giddy up, Gee up – there is no doubt that the name stuck, imprinted on the child's memory. Apart from caning, pupils were detained 'to work their school lessons again'. Cautions were followed by lectures, usually given on a Friday morning from 9.30-10.00 on Punctuality, Honesty, Thrift, Truthfulness, Kindness to animals and The Commandments. Some parents helped to enforce the discipline:

'...father brought him to school twice this week with his hands tied for playing truant'.

At Castle Cary in Somerset's Vale of Avalon, children who truanted from Sunday School were imprisoned for a suitable period in the parish lock-up, a round stone building with a roof shaped like a policeman's helmet, built in 1779 at a cost of £23.

28 Feb. 1898	Jesse Hughes caned for throwing stones at W. Harries, one of the teachers.
1 July 1901	Headmaster compelled to have a word with one of the Standard VI girls because she was bathing with sailors and she used foul language.

Ysgol Borthygest, Gwynedd

A parent on bringing her first child to school on my first day as a head teacher said, 'You won't smack her if she is naughty, will you? I would rather you told me and I will deal with it.' I pointed out that it was very unfair to punish a child at home for something done earlier in the day and that, in any case, I was not likely to smack her.

The same mother – on bringing her third child to school said, 'and if he needs a good hiding you have my full permission to give him one.'

Swarland, Northumb.

Sweeping timber lines of Swarland School in Northumberland

Social distinctions are often highlighted more by the children's own behaviour than any contrived classification of creed or class based on position and standing, as between the innocent and the inhibited.

One of our five year olds used to take his trousers off when it rained, to paddle in the puddles ... another child on his first day, having great trouble with his new trousers had them unbuttoned by his class teacher. I happened to meet him along the corridor clutching his trousers round his hips. He looked up and said, 'I say, I do look rather foolish don't I'.

Swarland, Northumb.

27 April 1882 — A boy in the third standard has been guilty of indirect falsehood. I gave him a punishment by working a short time after school hours, but deeming it better always to bring before my scholars the good qualities to be admired and wished for, I did not dwell too long upon the evil done, but rather tried to raise a wish for the opposite virtue. This I tried to do by reading the story of George Washington, dwelling particularly upon the love and affection given by a father to his erring but truthful son.

Coates, Glos.

18 Apr. 1878 — Flogged four boys for hooting outside the school.

4 Mar. 1881 — Several members of the Board came into school and complained that I did not thrash severely enough, though I have had several complaints from mothers for doing it.

Drayton Parslow, Bucks.

Corporal punishment is to be abolished in all maintained schools as from 15 August 1987. The use of corporal punishment after that date will remove the common law defence that the teacher was acting in *loco parentis*. Any teacher using corporal punishment would be liable to a civil action for battery ... By 'corporal punishment' is meant not only the use of the cane but also other forms of physical chastisement, such as the slapping or shaking of pupils or the throwing of missiles (e.g. chalk).

Extract from Section 46 of 1986 Education Act

A VILLAGE SCHOOL: THROUGH THE LOG BOOKS AND THE MEMORIES OF A CENTENARIAN

Filkins, a stone-built village in Oxfordshire, is by-passed by the A361 but sought out today by those attracted to its craft workshops complex and the George Swinford Museum. Housed in a seventeenth-century cottage next door to the old village lock-up, the museum is a tangible tangle of local, social, and domestic history caught up in the rusting man-traps and yellowed tallow candles, the

Filkins School: Fun on Sports Day

worn tools and the odds and ends of yesteryear – the collection of a remarkable man who celebrated his 100th birthday by publishing his recollections of the village, appropriately titled *The Jubilee Boy*. Schooldays stand out sharply in George Swinford's long memory of his 100-year-long life and it is his comments which intersperse the entries from the School Log Books and official reports and documents to draw up this picture of one village school throughout its life.

Broughton-cum-Filkins Church of England School was built to accommodate 112 pupils: there were but fifteen on roll when it closed in 1981 and the name was changed around, probably through assumption rather than official designation – Filkins Parish having absorbed Broughton hamlet by that time!

'There were about 105 children when I went to school. They came when they were 4, or when it was convenient for their mothers to send them – there wasn't much room in the cottages in those days for the big families. Then they left when they were about 12 or 13, some left before that if they were wanted at home to help out, or could earn a bit on the farm or in service. My father paid two pence a week to go to school, but that had stopped when I went.

'I was born in 1877, in Queen Victoria's Golden Jubilee year; the second of 12 children, I went to school when I was 4.'

The Committee of Council on Education agrees to the engagement of the scholar, Mary Jane Titchener (3rd Year) as a Pupil Teacher ... The most convenient hours, which circumstances permit, being fixed for the Pupil Teachers' lessons. At the close of each year, the Pupil Teachers are required to present certificates of good conduct from the Managers, and of punctuality, obedience, and attention to their duties from the schoolmaster or mistress. Certificates that the Pupil Teachers have been attentive to their religious duties are also required.

Privy Council Office, Downing Street, June 1868

Broughton-cum-Filkins School 1 July 1896

Mr Henry Lewis C. T. (Head)
Mrs H. J. Lewis
The Pupil Teacher H. J. Lewis must not be allowed to serve in school for more than 20 hours a week, as specified in paragraph 1 of the Memorandum of Agreement.

HMI Report, 1896

1896

7 Sept.	Re-opened school – 77 present
12 Oct.	Holiday – Filkins Feast
30 Nov.	The most irregular children are those coming from College Farm. When attending they are very seldom here till 9.15 or later.
	Sometimes we were late for school, but if we said we had been holding the doctor's horse all was well.
18 Dec.	A great many children away this afternoon chiefly because their mothers are gone to Bradwell Grove for gifts.

1897

19 Feb.	By order of the Medical Officer the school is closed for a month. There were between 60 and 70 children down with measles today.
15 Apr.	We are not making satisfactory progress yet, the debility following measles and chicken-pox the apparent cause.

'The Vicar used to give a shilling for the best drawing book. When I got into Standard 4 I won it, but the shilling was never paid to me.'

22 June	School closed that the children might attend the Diamond Jubilee Celebrations.

'We marched off from the school in the morning, some had proper flags and those that didn't carried a piece of red, white or blue rag to make out. There wasn't much red material about those days. I remember when old Squire Fox put his hunting jacket in the rummage sale, well, the women fought one another for it, though that was for a bit of brightness for the middle or the corners of the pegged rag rugs they made – but, anyway, we all managed to rustle up some bit of something or other to wave about on the day.

'We had all sorts of sports – running and jumping and tug-of-war. There were only four bikes in the village so they had to have several heats of the fast and slow cycle races. The women and all joined in. Then there was another lot of bread and cheese and meat. Oh, yes, people talked about the Jubilee for ever.'

The following is the List of Object Lessons proposed for 1897-8:

How Heat is produced	A Lighthouse	Leaves of Plants	The Globe
Mariner's Compass	An Errand Boy	Truthfulness	The Sea
Parts of a River	Day and Night	Cleanliness	A Ship
Stems of Plants	A Lifeboat	A Watch	A Train
Bamboos	Potatoes	A Book	Climate
Starch	Candles	Money	Rice
Pens	Soap	Mole	Bees
Roots	Air		

Recitations:

St. I-II	'The Village Blacksmith'	Longfellow	48 lines
St III	'Barbara Frietchit'	Whittier	60 lines
	'Casabianca'	Hemans	92 lines
	'The Inchcape Bell'	Southey	
St. IV-V	'The May Queen'	Tennyson	106 lines
	'The Ship on Fire'	Mackay	
St. VI	'Marmion and Douglas'	Scott	164 lines
	'The May Queen'	Tennyson	

'I started off fitting in well – I was interested in everything, but there was not a lot going on. I remember one of the recitations we learnt –

King Bruce of Scotland flung himself down
In a lonely mood to think,
True, he was a monarch and wore a crown
But his heart was beginning to sink.'

The Master of this School has infused a considerable amount of energy into his pupils and has taught them to speak up ... The higher grant for the class subject is recommended with hesitation. It is to be hoped that his grant will be more fully earned next year. Simultaneous answering ought to be forbidden in all classes. A proper urinal is badly needed; also materials for illustrating object lessons.
Infant Class: their slate work is less satisfactory than their oral work ... on the whole the school bids fair to make good progress under its painstaking and intelligent teacher.

HMI Report, 11 Aug. 1897

1898

24 Jan.	Under Section 1 (4) of the Voluntary Schools Act a Grant of £25 made for the purpose of increasing salaries, affecting repairs, and providing additional apparatus.

'I was taught by the schoolmaster's wife until I was 6 or 7. We mostly sang hymns and learnt a few recitations. Then I went into Class One in the big room, we had iron seats with planks on them, and ink-wells with brass tops on chains (I believe I've got one in the Museum). If you slid along the plank to get out, you got a splinter in your backside.'

10 May	Geography lessons last fortnight – Midland counties, London, Oxfordshire, own vicinity and Balkan Peninsula.
19 May	The Managers now supply us with 13 copies of *The Scholars' Own* monthly and the children in the upper classes seem greatly to appreciate the change.
1 June	Six boys and girl gone to Witney to be examined for the Labour Certificates.
20 June	The adoption of drawing upon paper instead of on slates has led to a very satisfactory improvement in care and cleanliness.
26 Sept.	Holiday – Burford Fair.

1899

20 Feb.	Mr and Mrs R. Carter sent to prison and the three children to the workhouse.
6 Mar.	Ada James now acting as Monitress (Probationer) and therefore her name taken off the Register.

Withdrawals:

Caleb Ebsworth	12.7.1893	Proficiency certificate
Lucy Robey	11.9.1893	Dead
Juliana Church	21.12.1893	Wanted at home
Jessie Lewis	22.2.1895	Appointed as Monitress
Robert Ebsworth	27.2.1896	Incurable it is believed – to be re-admitted if recovers
John Francis	9.6.1897	Dead

Admission Register 1893-7

28 Apr.	There being a doubt where Ada James could fairly compete for the Bishop's prize – being a paid monitor – the matter was referred to the Diocesan Inspector, who

decided that, having received her lessons as a scholar in the class during the year, she could.

'The parson came down nearly every day to give us our scripture lesson. We had to learn the collect and a verse of a hymn. We got 3 marks on the register – one for attendance, one for the collect and one for the verse.

'These were counted up at the end of the year, and perhaps you got a prize. When we attended (Choir) it was marked on the register and we received a halfpenny, which was paid out at Christmas. If you disbehaved at any of the services, the parson would say "Swinford, you will be docked". This meant you lost your halfpenny.'

5 June	George Swinford continues his disobedient conduct and impudence, for which he has, this day, been caned. His example was followed by Fred Flux, whose conduct has, hitherto, been good.

An older person should be appointed to scrub and dust the school daily

Sub Inspector HMI, 22 June 1899

'The bigger boys were appointed each week to light the fires in the winter and sweep and dust the rooms. This meant an hour before school and an hour after, for which we received two pence a week.'

14 July	Half holiday – Broughton Sunday School Treat.
2 Oct.	A woman has now been engaged to sweep and dust the school daily.
24 Oct.	George Swinford again giving trouble by beating and swearing at other children.

'Now and then the magic lantern man used to come to our school. I remember his cork leg, which squeaked. We used to be naughty and throw our caps at the screen. He had a carbide lamp and the gas leaked into the gully which ran under the school doorstep. One day I threw a match into it and it exploded and cracked the step. You can still see the crack.'

1900

14-15 Feb.	School closed owing to the deep snow.
22 Feb.	A very long list of absentees sent to the School Attendance Committee, who seem to care less and less for the great irregularity. The weather is now fine and free from snow. Number away this beautiful day – 22
9 Mar.	Children now irregular who used to be most regular.
31 May	This morning we heard of the capture of Pretoria, so at 11.30 the National Anthem was sung and the children allowed to go home.

The lower standards are still restless and inattentive and they contain some backward children; the strain of teaching and controlling such children ought not to be thrown on a girl of 14. There are entries in the Log Book which show that moral training and conduct are matters of considerable difficulty here, and this is another reason for strengthening the staff. The offices arrangements are still unsatisfactory. The pail system has not been adopted, nor so far as I could see, have the closets been cut off from the cesspool. I am to point out the Grant last year was allowed on the express understanding that the recommendations would be carried out.

HMI Report, August 1900

1901

6 Jan. Thermometer registered 46°F in classroom.

10 May Had serious talk with children regarding state of their heads, because many complaints received from parents. Having myself seen yesterday lice crawling in E. C's hair, I, without mentioning names, begged of all girls to thoroughly wash and comb out their hair upon reaching home.

It has become impossible to declare the school efficient. The necessary improvement is not likely to be made unless the Managers will appoint an Assistant Teacher who can govern children as well as teach them, Reading is still taught by unintelligent methods. The mistress should visit a good infant school in order to study good methods of teaching reading. The desks on the gallery should be replaced by others of suitable height and good construction. I am directed to give the Managers formal warning under Article 86 that the next Annual Grant may be withheld under that Article if, after his next visit, he again reports the School to be inefficient.

HMI Report, 14 Aug. 1901

8 Nov. The children who are reported as irregular week after week are becoming notorious for their dishonesty and foul language.

1902

'One day I was given a thrashing which wasn't needed, and when the master went to put the stick away in the desk, I ran up the school and opened the door. The children called "He's run, Sir". I got my cap and away I went, up College Hill where some bigger boys were ploughing. I walked up and down with them until dinner time, and then I went to Mr Holloway, the blacksmith, and blew the bellows for him. He asked why I was not at school, and then I said "I runned off" and that was the end of my schooling.'

2 June Gave children a half holiday this afternoon, because news received of the Proclamation of Peace.

23 June	School was to be opened today to complete the requisite number of attendances and the remainder of the week given as a Coronation Holiday.

1903

18 May	Christine Trinder brought message that brother Kenneth very ill in bed – he and his brother amusing themselves with barrow and spades in garden all day.
19 May	Same as yesterday as regards latter portion of last remark.
6 July	Dorothy Flux, aged 12, who has obtained the Labour Certificate by passing Standard V, commenced her duties as Monitress in the Infants room today.
12 Oct.	Filkins Feast. School closed as usual for the day.

1904

8 Jan.	School closed for Entertainments to be given for 2½ days.
13 Jan.	We have not yet received goods asked for on Oct 14. Received only ½ gallon of ink for upper school and are almost out of it.
20 Jan.	The Physical Exercises have had to be carried on within the Schoolrooms nearly all the winter, the wet weather and the state of the playground forbidding it out of doors.
18 Mar.	E.Lawrence and B. Glover have not attended school for several *years*.
6 May	Fires discontinued in Sunday School on April 17 and in the Day School on May 5.
6 June	Object Lessons in Botany just now include practical instruction in budding and grafting, the season just commencing for such garden work. From the requests for buds these will soon increase the variety of roses in the cottage gardens of the parish.

Scheme of work proposed for 1904

Object Lessons:	Infants: Money, Letter, Steel Pen, Slate, Umbrella, Brick, Table, Basket, Outside of House, Tallow Candle, Cat, Cow, Dog, Elephant, Lion, Camel, Apple, Cotton, Wild Flowers.	
Recitations:	Sts. III-VII	The Bridge (Longfellow)
		May Queen (Tennyson)
	St. I-II	A Noble Boy
		Father's Return
	Infants	Brownie's Punishment
		A Penny to Spend

26 Sept.	School closed for the annual fairs at Burford and Langford, as usual.
7 Nov. to 2 Jan.	School closed by Medical Officer – measles epidemic. The recommendations in HMI's Report have been attended to – the gallery of the classroom has been removed and new desks substituted; an experienced, and apparently capable, supplementary teacher has been appointed to take charge of the Infants. In addition, the classroom has been provided with mammoth letters, wands and flags to make the Physical Exercises more varied and interesting, and things begin to look brighter already. The school has also been nicely white-washed and re-painted during the holidays.
24 Mar.	Alice Cox brought child 2 years old to be 'minded' whilst mother was out; sent home at close of school and it was not to be repeated. Did same next day and child sent home at noon. When tried on a third time sent home at once. Mrs Morris also, next week, tried some dodge and kept elder girl away four times.
31 Mar.	Mr Cox of Langford Downs kept his daughter Alice away because little boy not kept here to be 'minded' whilst mother out.

Object Lessons – Upper Division:

In addition to the Lessons based on Snelgrove's Botany and Thomson's Rambles, 10 or 12 lessons suitable to the district, such as Haymaking, Harvest, Turnip and other weeding, Gardening, Cheese and Butter-making.

1905

11 July	The hay is plentiful, making much work, and causing some irregularity. It seems, now that the harvest is more quickly gathered in than formerly, that the harvest holidays might be curtailed by a fortnight, and a fortnight's holiday given at hay-making instead.
24 Nov.	Upon making complaint to the School cleaner of the dirty state of the floor and forms lately was told that it was owing to the fact that she had to come and sweep by lantern light after choir-practices and Band of Hope meetings had been held in the room.
28 Nov.	A Missionary Address instead of Scripture Lesson this morning.
1 Dec.	The School has been occupied four evenings this week. Gave the Vicar a copy of the Education Act this morning.
4 Dec.	Owing to repeated interference by (the Vicar), one of the Managers, I have been compelled to tender my resignation of the Mastership of this School, after nearly 15 years service.

9 Dec. The Vicar has desired me not to interfere for the purpose of keeping order whilst he is teaching, but to leave it to him. I had stopped those eating apples, mocking during devotions, and showing want of respect to him.

21 Dec. At Band of Hope Meeting on Nov 29 the school harmonium knocked over and damaged. Asked Correspondent (the Vicar) to have it repaired. Last evening at 2.15 he called, looked at it, denied that it was broken when knocked over by Dorothy Flux, and refused to have it put right, so I cannot use it for music lessons nor to accompany songs.

1906

9 Jan. This morning at 9 o'clock Christopher Clack was told to stand out of his class for a short time as a punishment for misconduct in the playground. At 9.07 the Vicar came in and ordered the boy back to his class. To this I objected, as being a direct incentive to disobedience to my orders, and I made the boy remain in front of his class.

11 Jan. Mr Elford visited the School taking measures and photographing. The subject of the friction over the Vicar's proceedings was discussed and the Vicar given clearly to understand that the discipline of the school is in the hands of the Head Teacher who is responsible therefore to the Managers and the Education Committee. At the same time, the Teacher said that, as usual, he would do nothing to interfere with the Vicar in the conduct of his Scriptural Instruction. The Bible is never read at *these lessons* now.

14 Feb. On Friday, Monday and yesterday, as the Vicar did not come, I took the Scripture Lessons and found a great falling off in the knowledge. This is, I consider, owing to want of system and departures from the time-table. The children told me the Shepherds followed the Star and went to Herod, etc, etc.

The Managers expressed regret that the Headmaster had thought fit to make entries regarding the Vicar of Filkins, and cannot associate themselves with them.

Minutes of Managers' Meeting, 23 Feb 1906

2 Mar. Henry Lewis ceased to hold the Mastership at this date. Term of recorded service in this school: 2 Feb 1891 – 2 March 1906.

5 Mar. I, Thomas Francis Airey, commenced my duties as Headmaster in these schools today. On the same date my wife, Maggie Evelyn Airey, commenced as Assistant

	Teacher. Mrs Marion Louise Harris (Assistant) Dorothy Flux (Monitress) Number on roll 97.
9 Mar.	After a week's experience in the school, I must state that the discipline and general behaviour of the children are very unsatisfactory. The attendance has been very good, much better than for many weeks previously; whether this is from a desire to see the new master, or the beginning of a permanent improvement remains to be seen.
19 Mar.	All the children present all day with the exception of one baby.
7 May	A chain was affixed to the School bell.
1 June	Gave out monthly tickets for perfect attendance during May. 68 tickets earned this month.
12 June	This morning, during first registration during which time the school door is always locked, the Vicar came to the door. He rattled the latch, and knocked loudly on the door. When the monitress opened it, as usual before prayers, he came in stating in a loud voice that it was the second time he had been locked out, and that the door should not be locked. I answered that it was the rule of the school. I am writing I. Elford re above incident today.
6 July	The attendance this week has been remarkably good, notwithstanding that 'haytime' has begun.
2 Aug.	This evening the children assisted by a number of local artistes gave a concert to raise funds for a school treat. In spite of a violent thunderstorm the room was crowded and we had a most successful concert. After paying the expenses, we shall have nearly £2 10s for the treat.
15 Oct.	Today is Filkins Feast. There has always been a whole holiday for this. This year it was decided to abandon this, and for the present year substitute a half holiday.
2 Nov.	Writing in Infant Room is faulty. Pens are lifted after each letter and in most cases O's are joined on left.
30 Nov.	The Oxfordshire County Council have given formal permission for a school garden.

Much improvement has been made in this school by the new teachers. The discipline is now good, and the exercise books very neat. While the work is carefully planned and intelligent methods are used.

HMI Report, 5 Dec 1906

1907

10 Jan.	Gardening lesson in afternoon. New tools used for first time.
15 Jan.	Received a bundle of trees for garden and a rain gauge.
18 Jan.	Children photographed this afternoon.
22 Feb.	Received 2 loads of manure.

26 Mar. Received goods from Charles and Dible, also a note to say a parcel was at Lechlade Station. A man stating himself to be a broken down army schoolmaster called at the school today soliciting charity.

2 May Not being able to work comfortably with the Vicar I have this day handed in my resignation as Master of this School after 14 months' service.

This notice is that there are several sections in this book which are at variance with the purpose for which it is provided (e.g. 26 March and 2 May). The Log Book is no place for personal remarks or items of general interest (or otherwise). Attention is called to the Code of Regulation by Board of Education (Schedule 4) and to S.22 App.C of the Education Act, which lay down quite clearly what the scope of the entries should be, and in future this ruling must be strictly adhered to.

Capt. Wahab, Manager.

1 July George Bramwell commenced as Headmaster.

16 Sept. Miss Hardcastle made cocoa for the dinner children.

9 Oct. This morning I took the boys a march out along the Alvescot Road. They enjoyed it and it did them good.

31 Oct. The School team played their first football match this afternoon in Capt Wahab's field; after the game Mrs Wahab kindly entertained the players with tea and plumcake.

1908

21 Jan. A keen, frosty morning. Temperature of large room 35°. Several of the children complained of, and were shivering with, cold. Unfortunately, only one fire.

14 Feb. This evening 24 Infants were entertained to tea by the Master.

19 Mar. Received the official Punishment Book from the Vicar, who is the Chairman of the School Managers.

25 Mar. Headmaster ill absent from school.

2 June The Vicar in charge.

10 June Mr F Dawson commenced duties as Head Teacher.

18 Sept. A menagerie passing through the village this morning, instead of the usual scripture lesson, the children were allowed to go out and see the procession. A subsequent talk about elephants and camel showed that the children had used their eyes well.

6 Oct. News brought to the school this morning that the Rev M Scott Lawrence died last night.

21 Oct. Received box from Education Committee containing cards and forms for use in connection with medical inspection of children. Began fires in school.

Filkins School: Formal group, 1909

1909

23 Sept.	By request of the Managers the school was closed this afternoon for a concert held to help defray the cost of repairing the playground.
12 Nov.	This afternoon the Vicar brought into school a Time-indicating Cylinder.
25 Nov.	Mr Lawrence called, he brought half a gallon of seed potatoes for the school garden.
2 Dec.	The girls were invited to bring their own garments that need repair for the needlework lesson, but only one girl did so. The mothers seemed to object and said they prefer to do their own children's mending.

1910

20 May	Today, being the occasion of the funeral of His late Majesty, King Edward VII the School was closed for the afternoon in order that all might attend the memorial service held in the church.

1911

20 Jan.	A bench with three enamelled basins has been fixed in the classroom to the school for the children to wash their hands in when necessary. Two soap dishes and two rollers for towels are also provided.
28 Nov.	Medical Officer visited to examine the heads of the children previously found to be verminous. Twelve are

declared to be still dirty and excluded from school for one week.

1912

12 Feb. A new piano has been placed in the school, supplied by Mr A. W. Kempster of Fairford. At present the instrument is only on approval.

17 Apr. As there was a partial eclipse of the sun the children were taken out of doors to observe it and discuss it. Pieces of smoked glass were provided.

19 Apr. The piano has been finally purchased. The money was partly raised by subscriptions on the initiative of Mrs Woodhouse of The Yews. The Education Committee adding the sum of £7.

1914

7 Sept. This morning, in place of the ordinary arithmetic and reading lessons, the Head Teacher gave an address on the causes which have led to the European War and the reasons why this country is taking part in it.

9 Sept. Roy Giles, top boy in this school, has been successful in obtaining a Free Place in Witney Grammar School.

4 Nov. Roy Giles was the recipient of a silver watch awarded by the Education Committee for perfect attendance and good conduct for 9 years. The presentation was made by J N Hardcastle Esq.

10 Nov. This is the first time girls have been included in the gardening class.

1915

19 Mar. Charles Temple who is not legally entitled to be away from school, has been at work for 3 days at Broughton Hall Farm owing to the scarcity of labour created by the war.

15 Sept. Physical exercises were performed under difficulties this morning; wasps are numerous, and they worry children and teachers a good deal.

23 Dec. Certificates were given in place of the usual book prizes which the children voluntarily relinquished as a war economy.

1916

14 Feb. Two children from London admitted this morning. Their mother is engaged in making munitions for the war so they have come to stay in Filkins for a time.

11 May	Last night a very successful concert was given by the school children to aid the Oxford Red Cross Fund and the NUT War Aid Fund. A Total of £7 was raised.
3 July	Miss Hodgson, Organising Instructress in Domestic Subjects to the Oxfordshire Education Committee called to arrange for a lecture on Cottage Cookery and Economy in Food.
11 Sept.	Muriel Cotton has obtained, after a competitive examination, a free place in Witney Grammar School (the third scholar to do so in three years).

Filkins School, Oxfordshire, as at 16 Oct 1916:

No. on books:	80 in 2 Rooms
Average attendance:	5%
Wear and Tear:	15%
Correspondent:	J. N. Hardcastle, Broughton Hall
Care Com Sec:	Rev A. S. C. Austen
School Doctor:	C. T. Cheatle, Burford
Health Visitor:	Nurse Ward, New Yatt Road, Witney
Attendance officer:	E. W. Hyde, Bampton
Cleaner:	Mary Ann Puffitt. Scheduled duties 12/- monthly, includes special cleaning and washing dusters.

		Born	*Gross Annual Salary*
Head Teacher:	Frederick Dawson*	1871	£110
Teacher:	Ivy C. Giles	1893	£35
Teacher:	Mrs Elizabeth Giles	1883	£45
Monitress:	Mary S. Tinson	1903	£6

* over age for war service — Staff suffice for 75

15 Dec.	There have been very severe frosts during the last few days. By pouring water on smooth parts of the playground excellent slides were made for the children and instead of working through ordinary tables of physical exercises they were allowed to slide under the supervision of the Master and teachers, who themselves took part in the game.

1917

7 June	As there is a good deal of work to be done in the garden, and as the supply of drawing paper has to be severely restricted at present, all the older boys, whether belonging to the gardening class or not, were taken to work in the garden. A lesson was given on the Woolly Aphis.

3 July — The Vicar of Filkins will not give his usual Religious Instructions for an indefinite period, having been appointed a chaplain to His Majesty's Forces.

10 July — Instead of drawing, the boys sprayed the potato crops with Burgundy mixture.

18 Sept. — The children have had a half holiday for the purpose of picking blackberries for the army and navy. Accompanied by the Master and Teachers, they gathered 64 lbs of fruit. (4 half days granted for this purpose.)

1918

19 Sept. — 169 lbs blackberries dispatched (from yesterday's picking)

1919

11 Feb. — The Vicar has returned to the Parish (after war service).

9 Apr. — Dr Laws, dental surgeon, (of Milton-under-Wychwood) inspected the teeth of all the children between the ages of 6 and 11.

17 July — In place of gardening the children wrote out a large number of notices and programmes in connection with the Peace Celebrations to be held in Filkins on Saturday.

19 July — (Saturday) The children assembled at the school at 2.30 when J N Hardcastle Esq, Chairman of the Managers, presented each child with a medal commemorating peace.

11 Nov. — At 11 a.m. read the King's Proclamation and to see that the two minutes silence were observed in accordance with His Majesty's wishes in commemoration of the Armistice signed a year ago today.

1920

9 Jan. — A lecture on the navy was given in the Institute on this date by Admiral Sir Edward Bradford. It was most interesting and illustrated by lantern slides. About 30 of the older scholars sang beautifully several patriotic sea songs besides taking part in a tableau representing Britannia, her Dominions and Allies. The proceeds are to go towards establishing a school library.

16 Feb. — The new School Library was opened this afternoon. Books may be borrowed from Standard II upwards, and also by former scholars up to the age of 16. A penny a month will be paid by each child as it is thought that children value more what they themselves contribute to.

Several sets of indoor games such as draughts, chess, ludo and puzzles have been purchased for the children's use during the dinner hour on wet days.

19 Feb. This afternoon the children of the gardening class did two hours work double digging and manuring their plots.

26 Mar. Absence excuses not very satisfactory, being spring cleaning and minding baby.

30 Mar. This being Holy Week, the Vicar will not give his usual religious instruction in school.

This school is in the hands of a capable, keen and thoughtful headmaster. The infants are taught with care and good sense by their new teacher, but she should cultivate greater brightness of manner.

HMI Report, 3 May 1920

25 June Mr Hoskins has kindly given permission to use the meadow opposite the school for organised games on Friday afternoons under the supervision of the Master and Teachers. The infants will play from 3-3.30; the older children from 3.30-4 p.m. A new time-table will be submitted to His Majesty's Inspector.

1921

22 Dec. Ten shillings was today sent to the Radcliffe Infirmary, Oxford. This sum having been subscribed by the children during the year.

1922

22 Nov. Received an iron kettle for boiling water for making hot drinks for the children who take their dinner at school.

28 Nov. Received 5/- from Mrs E Radband in respect of spectacles supplied to Ruby through the School Medical Service.

1923

26 Apr. School closed in accordance with His Majesty's wishes to celebrate the marriage of HRH the Duke of York and the Lady Elizabeth Bowes-Lyon.

1924

15 Jan. Miss MacDonald, School Health Visitor, inspected the children today. She left 3 dozen tins of toothpaste for their use, the charge of 1d a tin and ½d for refils.

26 June — A number of children whose teeth were found defective were treated today in the Church House, which is near the school.

17 July — The school was closed today in order that the Master and Teachers might take a party to the British Empire Exhibition at Wembley.

23 July — George Swinford 11 years of age, and Eva Giles, 12, have been awarded Free Places at Witney Grammar School.

1925

29 Apr. — The boys of Standard VII have made drawers to fit their desks so that they can have all their books, pens, pencils etc always to hand. The drawers were made from drawings previously done by the boys themselves.

5 Oct. — Eight girls started a course at the Broadwell Cookery Centre.

1926

18 June — For a few weeks the meadow available for games is closed until hay-making is completed, so games have to be played at the school playground which is not really so convenient as the ball frequently gets into a neighbour's garden.

1927

8 Feb. — Mrs Goodenough talked for some time to the children about the historical pictures she has given. There are 12 altogether and include Harold's last stand at Senlac and The Death of Wolfe.

15 Mar. — The Rev Austen has very kindly given 10/- to provide glass for the frames which the boys are making for the pictures presented on Feb 8. No. on roll 75.

1928

11 Jan. — Received completion of order for science materials for elementary science lessons.

20 Jan. — Work examined in bookbinding and basketry.

10 Feb. — This morning three children were examined under the new scheme for scholarships. All were girls. The examination was carried out in strict accordance with the regulations of the Education Committee. The first part was a Reading Test, the second was a Primary

	Intelligence Test. The Head Master acted as Supervisor and Mrs Dore as time-keeper.
7 May	Mrs Goodenough of Filkins Hall has arranged that for the summer months each child shall have half a pint of new milk daily. What was left of the 4½ gallons supplied was given to the children who remained at school for dinners.
4 July	Mrs Goodenough called this morning to see whether the children appreciate the milk she so kindly supplies for their use.

1931

18 Mar.	Today the Master was at Langford School assisting in the supervision of the Part II of the Scholarship Examination, with 3 candidates from Filkins – Freda Swinford, Arthur Melluish and Joan Perry, (All were successful in passing for Burford Grammar School).
24 Mar.	Today the old long desks were sold; three belonging to the Managers, four to the Education Committee, they sold for 3 shillings each.

1932

29 June	Mr Blore and Mr Day from the Education Office to consult with the Head Teacher regarding the books and furniture to be transferred to the new Senior School at Langford after the Summer holidays when it is proposed to convert this school to a Junior School.

This school is commendable for several reasons. The atmosphere is the right one for a church school, the children are devout and well mannered. The lessons are being well driven home, the text of the Bible being often quoted.

Diocesan Report, 28 July 1932

5 Sept.	Today the school reopened under changed conditions. Henceforth it will be Filkins Junior School. Twenty-seven children of 11 years of age and over have been transferred to Langford Central School. The staff now consists of the Head Teacher, Mr F Dawson, and Miss Marmont, uncertificated Teacher. The number now on the Admission Register is 46.

1935

16 Sept.	The school was closed today as nearly all the children go to Witney Feast. A greater proportion go now as motor bus facilities are greater and the fares cheap.

9 Oct. Miss Bezzant weighed the children who have milk at school daily and all had improved in health.

This school was decapitated in 1932 when its senior pupils were transferred to the new school at Langford. It now has 41 children ranging from 4 to 10 years. The Head Master, who has entered on the last year of his long and very honourable service, has adjusted himself well to his new conditions.

HMI Report, 1 Dec. 1935

1936

21 Jan. HM King George died last night.

22 Jan. All children went to The Institute from 10-10.45 a.m. to hear by radio the proclamation of the Accession of King Edward VIII.

1937

5 Apr. Today several children had Horlicks Malted Milk in place of the 1/3 pint of new milk.

11 May Tomorrow being the Coronation of HM King George VI there will be 3 days holiday to commemorate the event in accordance with the King's wish.

1939

11 Sept. Seven children evacuated from Hallsville School, Canning Town, accompanied by an assistant master Mr Wilkens. Eleven other children admitted who are staying in Filkins on account of the War.

12 Sept. The Vicar agreed to the use of a room in the Church Room as a classroom (for the evacuees).

1940

14 Apr. School reopened (during Whitsun holiday) in accordance with the orders broadcast by the Board of Education. This is on account of the serious war situation consequent upon the German invasion of Holland.

20 June Sixteen children evacuated from Randal Cremen School, Shoreditch, bringing the numbers to 60.

2 July Miss Morgan, a LCC teacher who accompanied the evacuees arrived to help in the school. We shall, therefore, use the Carter Institute which the Trustees kindly offered us.

30 Aug. School closed for 1 week's summer holiday.

1941

30 Apr.	The whole school went for a nature walk and collected dandelion roots for the Red Cross.
12 Aug.	Immunisation of children against diphtheria carried out today.
25 Oct.	This was War Weapons week in the village and during the week the total raised by the School Saving Association was £324.

1942

21 Jan.	Thirteen children only this morning due to deep snow, ten of them being evacuees from the Witney Clearing House. They were kept at school and given individual attention.
4 May	Enquiries made to see what accommodation is available for a school canteen.
14 Aug.	School broke up for summer holidays. It was left in such a condition, ie all books packed away so that the building could be put in use as a Rest Centre if the occasion should require it.

1943

30 Mar.	School Canteen opened today, 25 children partaking of dinner.
22 Apr.	A presentation (of a cheque) was made to Miss Nobbs (the LCC teacher) who has been with us since December 1940 on behalf of the school, the church and the village as a whole.

1944

11 Sept.	School closed for potato harvest holidays (2 weeks).

1945

30 Apr.	Mrs A Webster and Miss Louisa Reynolds, Cook and Assistant Cook at our School Canteen since its beginning, resigned today as they are returning to their homes in London. Mrs Deaney and Mrs Noakes take their place.
8-9 May	School closed VE Day, being public holiday on account of Germany's surrender to the Allies.
5 July	Children of 8 upwards began swimming lessons today. They will go every Thursday afternoon.

1946

9 May — Mrs Cripps gave a singing lesson this afternoon.

9 Sept. — During the holidays electric light has been installed.

1947

20 Nov. — School closed for wedding of HRH Princess Elizabeth and the Duke of Edinburgh. A tea-party was held in the Institute for the children.

1948

26 Apr. — Half holiday this afternoon, being the Silver wedding of Their Majesties the King and Queen.

6 May — Today being Ascension Day, the children attended church at 9 a.m. returned to school for their milk and then the rest of the day was a holiday (as previous years).

15 Nov. — The Union Jack was flown and the National Anthem sung to commemorate the birth of a son to HRH the Princess Elizabeth last night, Sunday, November 14.

1949

7 Sept. — During the holidays water has been laid on to the school. Three wash-basins fitted with running water and flush lavatories have been installed.

1951

10 Mar. — The appointment of Mrs Deaney as Cook-Caterer, she has up to now held the position of Cook – the Catering having been done by Head Teacher.

1952

15 Feb. — Today at 2 p.m. the two minutes' silence was observed in school, as everywhere else in the country, in memory of King George VI, whose funeral was taking place at that time at Windsor. The children were able to follow the Service on the wireless.

10 June — Fifteen children were taken to the Village Museum, Mr George Swinford very kindly gave up the afternoon to showing them around and talking about the exhibits.

8 Sept. — Seven children transferred to Burford Comprehensive

School, this being the year of change from Langford to Burford.

1953

4 June — School re-opened after 3 days' holiday to commemorate the Coronation. A large photograph of the Queen has been received as a gift from Education Committee and also a very beautiful Bible.

13 Oct. — Mrs Cripps brought a gramophone to school – a present from the whole family.

7 Dec. — This afternoon friends and parents attended a Sale of Work. There were two stalls, one the Managers (cakes, needlework, etc) and the children's (handwork, calendars and gifts).

1958

24 June — Mr Robin Tanner HMI called this afternoon for a few minutes to bid us farewell. Mrs Cripps spent an hour at school in commemoration of our new piano. She gave a most interesting talk on the pianoforte and on composers with selections from their music. Later the children wrote letters of thanks to Mrs Cripps for all she has done for our music and all brought flowers from their garden to make a large bunch to take to her home.

24 June — This afternoon the whole school were entertained by

Filkins School: In class in the 1950s

Mrs Cripps in her garden. Miss Goschen brought 12 children from her school (Eastleach) and they gave a display of country dancing – in which we joined later. After tea we had a sing-song in the drawing room.

25 July — The last day of term and the day of my retirement as Head Mistress of the School. A presentation of a very beautiful antique bureau and chair together with bouquets from the Juniors and Infants. Overwhelmed, I endeavoured to express my deep appreciation of the kind thought which had planned such a wonderful gift.

1959

8 July — As a consolidation to the cookery lessons in the Infants room, 19 parents sat down to tea on the lawn today. Cakes, scones and jam, all made by the Infants, were on the menu.

23 July — School Sports held. Over 40 mothers attended, plus friends and Managers. Notification received today that the School was granted Controlled status.

1962

5 Mar. — Work commenced on the conversion of the adjoining allotments into a school playing field.

1963

14 June — School closed at noon as Miss Moly and I took the 8 older girls to Weston for a camping week-end.

28 June — Took the junior boys for camping week-end at Weston.

1964

20 Feb. — Dr S Briggs came to talk to the children about folklore.

3 Nov. — Mr W Dreghorn, a geologist, came and took a party of children with me to a local quarry.

4 Nov. — Dr Grounds Peace came to talk to the children about the skeleton.

1965

22 June — TV production team came at 8.45 a.m. with HMI Walter Drabble to make film for 'Discovery and Experience' series.

1966

20 June	Mr Cole, Director of Education for Victoria in Australia, spent the day with us.
5 July	24 children were invited to live at the Froebel Institute in London for 5 days, giving demonstrations to the students in drama, music, movement, history and local studies.
6 Sept.	The 9 children who are in their last year will study French.
28 Oct.	A coffee evening to raise money for a new cooker was held. £26 12s 6d was raised.
29 Nov.	As an experiment, and an extension of the idea of our 7 schools working as a unit, a joint Managers Meeting was held at Langford School.

1967

17 July	Princess Dusdi, from Thailand, who was studying English education spent the afternoon here.

1968

31 May	The Juniors watched the opening of the Filkins by-pass.

1969

25 Nov.	School was closed this morning as teaching staff withdrew from duty on the request of the NAS and NUT Unions.

1970

16 Mar.	Parents were invited to school in the evening to view and discuss the BBC Radiovision programmes on Sex Education.
18 June	School closed because of the General Election. The large classroom was required as a polling station.
2 Nov.	Ordnance Survey office called to measure the school area and to receive sanction for the school name to appear on the next edition of the Ordnance Survey maps.

1971

25 Sept.	I took the school team to the County Cycling Proficiency Finals in Oxford. David Swinford was adjudged the best boy in the county.

1972

1 May	We held May Day celebrations in school. Dancing round the may-pole and a procession through the village.
20 Nov.	The school was closed to celebrate the Silver Wedding anniversary of Her Majesty the Queen and Prince Philip.

1973

21 Sept.	Number on roll 36.
11 Oct.	After school I went round to see George Swinford, senior about a proposed visit to his museum.
14 Nov.	Wedding of Princess Anne and Mark Phillips. The school was closed for the day.

1974

8 Jan.	After many days of constant sorting out of classroom materials and resources I arranged in the classroom a library corner and an art area. There are many good points about the school. It has a good atmosphere and the numbers in the classes facilitate individual help. Yet there is a real challenge to give the children of this delightful village a stimulating and exciting education to lift them above their past experiences and witness their full fruition! D. Holme [new Headmaster]
29 Jan.	Boys and I sorted out the gardening and games shed, finding plenty of rubbish and one or two treasures.
1 Feb.	The children have now settled down to a great degree. Initially I had found them excitable and rather fussy. This week we set up an 'interest table' with spring flowers. I also added one of my stuffed squirrels and one or two logs. I rather deplore the real lack of storage space in the school which tends to make for general untidiness. I have had to put stock into a room in the house. This is I feel rather an unsatisfactory state of affairs.
6 Feb.	Desks are old and we certainly should see about a television. Today was noteworthy for its snow. Children made snowmen in the paddock. I wheelbarrowed snow from school garden and was called in to lift the snowmen's heads on.
26 Feb.	During half-term I put up hessian on pinboarding and wood walls and purchased a William Morris fabric called the Mallow.

28 Mar.	New metric mathematics apparatus arrives. I can now scrap the old non-metric materials. Might be an idea to give it to our village museum!
29 Mar.	Delightful afternoon spent at Mr Cripps' Farm watching the lambing.
10 Apr.	We made a presentation to Mrs G Swinford (Auntie Doris) and Mrs I Monk (retiring kitchen staff) thanking them for loyal service to our school.
30 Apr.	Mr Wise makes curtains to go between infant and junior room. They are a William Morris Chrysanthemum Minor design.

'Sometimes William Morris came driving along the road from Kelmscott across the fields in his high carriage ... he always threw us a penny for opening the gate.'

6 May	Bill Asbridge brings a visitor and a dead fox.
5 June	The younger children's programme: 9.15-10.30 Mathematics 10.50-11.50 Writing and Reading Activities, including flash cards 1.30-2.30 Choosing Time eg Sand/Wendy corner. A story is read at the end of the day to the whole class. Sand and a Wendy Corner are new introductions to the room.
11 June	Dinner-time search for Eileen Wise's guinea pigs, 'Operation School children', in her garden. Successfully completed by every able-bodied boy.
5 Nov.	Excellent fire-work display and refreshments put on by parents.
12 Nov.	Second evening of Tuesday Club. We agreed to start at 6.30, finish at 8.30. The club is only run on the understanding that parents help.
14 Nov.	A double trip day. Took group with George Swinford to Farmington Quarry as a follow up on work done on Fox House which was re-roofed. In the afternoon visited Mr Long the hurdlemaker at Cote, near Bampton.
19 Nov.	Today I received new chairs and tables for junior room and so the pre-war and broken furniture removed. New tables are trapezoidal, some wooden, some formica. Also two new bin units in Tasmanian Oak. What a difference these make to classroom!
21 Nov.	Took children to Thame. They viewed the church and went to the Red House Bookshop which had its official opening in the new building. Here we met a living author – Noel Streatfeild (*Ballet Shoes*).
20 Dec.	End of term. Carpet arrived for school.
31 Dec.	School social New Year's Eve. Children played bells at midnight.

1975

4 Feb.	Bill Asbridge spends day with us on the theme of Gambia. What a time we had – small children dressed in Gambian costume, playing drums and wafting away imaginary flies with cow hair whisks.

...we discussed the place of French in our school and whether we should continue it. The National Foundation for Educational Research has brought out a report on the subject. After 10 years' research it states among other things that there are no substantial gains in teaching French before 11 years. We feel in the interest of our children that we should discontinue French in the near future.

Extract from letter to Parents 10 Feb. 1975

20 Feb.	Imperial Typewriter arrives.
7 May	Received duplicator on free loan.
9 May	Field trip to Brynberian in Mynydd Precelan for week.
5 June	Closed for Common Market Referendum.
24 Sept.	Played Brize Norton at football and netball.

1976

10 Feb.	Went to Lark Rise with material for exhibition at Museum of Modern Art.
21 July	BBC visit about children's programme 'Take a Ticket to' to be filmed in the village on August 2.

1977

7 Jan.	During last few weeks we have collected over 4000 stamps for the Blue Peter Appeal. Prizes were distributed to Tracy Hambridge (1020 stamps), Kevin (700) and Maria (400) stamps for children of Lebanon.
2 June	School Jubilee Party.
3 June	Many people in the village contributed to the (Jubilee) exhibition which reflected the last 25 years nationally and events in the village. School log books were on display. These caused great interest particularly from older people. Handicrafts were displayed, and work from Mr D. Trinder, the village blacksmith. The exhibition, because of the unexpected interest shown, opened 4 times.
26 Sept.	Jo Homan of Boys Town, India to talk about his work and show slides.
9 Dec.	As a result, by their own efforts, the children are running a stall in school on Friday – by baking cakes, making things, bringing along comics and old toys they

raised £22 towards a buffalo for the farm in India, one sheep and 4 banana trees.

1978

4 Nov. Attended conference on Saturday on the future of small schools, due to the drop in school population. We were encouraged about our future, but we should make our villages aware of the real value of village education.

9 Nov. Chief Education Officer visited the school and I feel we made great strides in convincing him of the great value of village schools.

24 Nov. Buffalo Stall – fund-raising for Boys Town.

18 Dec. This is the end of an era, where the Head has traditionally lived in the school house. However, I am determined that the School will not suffer.

1979

28 Feb. Notes for parents outlining school policy and request for parents to help in school with cooking, etc.

1 Mar. Offers of help from Parents to help in school good.

Filkins School: Forgotten in 1988

17 Oct.	School Open Day to celebrate International Year of the Child.
27 Nov.	Met parents concerning possible closure of our school. Majority in favour of closure.
29 Nov.	Public meeting in village hall about closure. In the main majority wish for closure as soon as possible.
10 Dec.	Juniors went tree planting with Lady Anne Cripps.

1980

4 Feb.	School dinners increased to 35p a day.
1 Apr.	My last day at Filkins School. Looking back over 6 years it has seen considerable changes ... each year has brought out of the children greater attainments ... a few parents have given very generously of their time and talents. I thank them for this. D. Holme.
21 Apr.	36 pupils on roll.
2 Sept.	Re-opened after Summer holidays with 14 on roll.

1981

13 Jan.	One new entrant.
9 July	Sports afternoon. Children's tea and presentations to staff and pupils. Governors, parents and friends of the School joined us to mark a happy end to the school year. The boys and girls were given books and a Royal Wedding beaker each to mark the closing of the school. Presentations were made to the staff, many of whom had given long and valuable service to the school, by Lady Goodenough on behalf of the parents and governors.
14 July	Library van visited to collect books.
15 July	Final Assembly to mark the end of the school year – and, indeed, the end of the life of Filkins-cum-Broughton School.

4 *The Village School at Play, Work and War*

GAMES

...Now he had conquered another step in life, the step which all real boys so long to make; he had got amongst his equals in age and strength ... he lived with those whose pursuits and wishes and ways were the same in kind as his own.

Tom Brown's Schooldays

The true country child is still a great observer of the countryside. He knows where the robin builds its nest and what creatures live in the stream, the field, hedge and wood and in the drystone walls. When his little sister finds fewer white violets on the hedgerow bank and Granny is hard put to getting enough 'pips' to fill the old milk measure to make Gramp's cowslip wine, he heaps contumely on the farmer's use of pesticides and fungicides, and blames the new builders for polluting the local brook so that plant leeches and red roundworms have taken the place of the mayfly and freshwater shrimps – and is surprised to find at secondary school that these things are wrapped up in an examination syllabus called Environmental Studies.

George Swinford of Filkins, properly in Oxfordshire but culturally of the Cotswolds, delved deep into his memories as he celebrated his hundredth birthday to recall his schooldays between Queen Victoria's Golden and Diamond Jubilees.

We boys always carried stones in our pockets, ready to hit anything that moved – many a dinner was won by having a stone in your pocket at the right time. Every village had its champion stone-thrower. Bill Dyer was a dab-hand and could stone a hare that the squire's Shooting party missed. I heard tell as he stood on Braddle (Broadwell) Bridge and threw a stone clean over the weathercock on the church steeple.

Bandy was the popular team game – a kind of hockey without goals or rules. Sticks were cut from the hedge with a knob or crook at the bottom, with a chunk of wood for the 'nunney'. Equal sides were picked and the nunney was knocked from hedge to hedge, with no regard to position. The only accepted rule, in what was usually a rough and tumble game, was that if a player was hampered by another standing in front of him he issued the warning 'turn Bummy'. 'If you didn't move then, he could clout you with his stick'.

More vicious team games, now lost to rule-regulated football, were the Cotswold 'sports' of pud-fighting and dwile-flonking. Pud is indistinguishable from mud so the best time for a fight was immediately following rain when the pud was sticky enough to scoop up and mould on to a whippy stick, cut from the hedgerow. When both sides had armed themselves with their messy weapons they flipped and catapulted the mud across a great divide with such deadly accuracy and disastrous effect that one side usually called 'feenigs' – the schoolboy's language for giving in – before the schoolmaster realised what was going on and gave victors and vanquished a taste of his own whippy stick.

Dwile-flonking was usually confined to village sports day: a kind of rounders, the dwile was a blown-up pig's bladder, flonked by a flat board. Both, by scale of their sadistic attack on the opposition, would make the Eton Wall Game pale into a mere courtesy of exchange.

These primitive battles using the weapons at their feet were never captured by the Victorian and Edwardian artists who portray the youth of their day bowling their hoops. An iron hoop from the village blacksmith cost a shilling, but it did have an iron hook attached so it didn't have to be beaten along; the girls usually had wooden hoops.

Marbles were universal. In the Cotswolds the prized marble, special either for its size or colour or ready identification, was the 'tawl'. Glass marbles were 'glassies'; small ones the 'cots'.

Follow Tawl was the game we played on our way to school, shooting down the ruts made by the cart wheels. You started by throwing a tawl in the rut. The one behind had the first shot. If he hit the tawl he won a cot. The next boy behind him had the next shot, and if he hit the tawl the first one had to give him the cot.

Knock-off was a kind of marbles skittles played under a wall. Ring Tawl was pitched in a circle drawn in the dust and the marbles shot from between the thumb and forefinger only. The rule of keeping the hand firmly on the ground was chanted:

Knuckle down, knuckle down,
All four fingers touch the ground.

Another centenarian, Henry Curtis, recalled the games of his schooldays in East Grafton in Wiltshire, when marbles were beyond the pocket of his family.

I think there were only about five marbles between the whole school, and we used to try to win them with buttons. A marble would be put in a scooped out hollow in the ground and we would throw a flat pebble at it. The one who got the nearest pebble to the marble would be paid in buttons by the rest in the game. Then he would have to kneel down and throw all the buttons together and if they all landed in the hole the winner got the marble. We used to get a jolly good hiding at home when our mothers found the buttons had been cut off her coat. If you had a marble in your pocket the whack on your backside didn't bother you none – but if you had just lost a precious marble then by-hyes 'twould make your eyes sting!

Buttons proper was a kind of pitch-and-toss game, the buttons were won or lost by tossing a block similar to a dice – letters marked out on the faces instead of spots – A: all (take all), P: put (put on) N: none, and so on. The order of tossing was decided by the closeness to the block that the competitors aimed their button from a distance line.

The little actor dons another part;
Filling from time to time his 'humorous stage'
With all the persons, down to palsied age,
That life brings with her in her equipage;
As if his whole vocation
Were endless imitation.

William Wordsworth

Children are great imitators and singing games following courtship and marriage have been enacted by children for centuries. Thought to date back to the Restoration, two rhyming games of the Cotswolds were resurrected by the late Canon Henry Cheales.

'Jenny' is a one-verse, girl picks boy act in which the weeping Jenny irrespective of her real name, turns tears to smiles. The key words of each line are repeated before proceeding to the next.

Jenny sits a'weeping on a fine summer's day.
Oh! tell me what you're weeping for.
She's weeping for her true love.
Oh! Jenny must forget him,
So come and choose another one.
Now Jenny will be married.

In the Little Rissington version of 'The Wind Blows High' the principals retain their own identity, and the tune changes to accommodate the different stanzas.

The wind, the wind, the wind blows high,
The rain comes scattering down the sky.

Jane is handsome, she is pretty,
She is the girl of Rissington City.
She goes a-courting – one two, three!
Please to tell me, who is he?

Kenny Smith says he loves her,
All the boys are wild about her!
Let the world say what they will,
Kenny Smith loves her still.

He takes her down the garden, sits her on his knee;
Says, 'My ducky darling, what'll we have for tea?
A china cup and saucer, a guinea golden ring,
A plate to put the porridge on; ding, dong, ding'.

Singing games where principals are encircled have ritualistic shades in their performance; the chanting ring of children are both audience and participants of the simple story played out within their own private magical circle. Probably the most universal of them all is 'The Farmer wants a Wife'. Sapperton schoolchildren enlarge on their version by giving a reason to each one rejected from the circle by appropriate observations: 'You are too flowery – short, tall, stripey, spotty, green or checky' – according to their dress or stature.

Skipping games so popular a half century ago, are fast disappearing from the school playgrounds. Little gaggles of girls used to entrance their cronies with predictions of their destiny, decided by the point at which they stopped mid-skip.

This year, next year,
Sometime, never.

Tinker, tailor
Soldier, sailor.
Rich man, poor man,
Begger man, thief.

Coach, carriage
Wagonette – or – fly.

Silk, satin
Muslin, rags.

Big house, little house
Pigsty, barn.

Catching games are national old-time favourites played along quiet country roads and small school playgrounds. Sheep and wolf is a favourite from Devon. The 'wolf' would stand on one side and call:

'Sheep, sheep, come home.'
The rest replied:
'The sheep have gone to Derbyshire,
And won't be back for many a year,
Sheep, sheep, go home' –

at which point they all ran across and those which were caught had to join forces with the wolf until the whole 'flock' had been turned into a pack of 'wolves'.

'What's the time, Mr Wolf?' seems to be quite universal, whereas 'London' is played more in Wales than England!

The girls of Godshill Primary School were so fascinated with the tale of Appuldurcombe House, the theme for multi-disciplinary studies inspired by the national Domesday project, that they turned the account of its history – written by Mrs Roma Hames, their headmistress – into a very complicated clapping and singing playground game.

Sirs, a merry tale I'll tell
If you chance to think it cheery
It is sure to please you well
If you do not find it dreary.
  'Tis a tale of Appuldurcombe
  A Benedictine Priory.
  Then came Ann and Sir James Worsley
  Started up a family tree
Three hundred years they ruled the valley
Built a fort called Worsley's Tower
Richard worked for fat King Henry
Now lies 'neath Godshill's church tower.
  Brother John lived most in London
  But when dead was brought back home
  Also lies in Godshill church
  Succeeded by brother Tom.
Richard Worsley, wise was he
By King James was made a knight,
Loved his books and studied deeply
Captain of the Isle of Wight,
  Then came Henry, then came Robert,
  Builder of the present house.
Next came James and then came Thomas
Then Sir Richard (and his spouse)
This was the last of all the Worsleys
To live in Appuldurcombe fine.
The house and all its treasures sold
The end of the ancient line.

Godshill girls devised their own clapping game to illustrate the history of the Worsley family

Then a school and now a ruin
Left to nature and the air
Still a noble lovely relic
Empty now but still so fair.

The ruined mansion in its 'Capability Brown' park is now taken over by English Heritage. The greatest mansion on the Isle of Wight, it was a Benedictine monastery before it was the ancestral home of the Worsley family – and the village school at Godshill has particular interest in its history as their school owes its foundation of 1615 to the Lady Ann. Few benefactors enjoy such active perpetuity.

Very small schools face problems in organised games if there are fewer pupils on roll than a rounders team. St Martin's School has no hard playground, but the freedom of open spaces and a spectacular view of all the Scilly Islands. The four children have to wait until the summer months when sea crossings are easier to join with the children from the other island schools for any competitive games and the annual combined off-islands school picnic on Samson, bare, barren and uninhabited for over a hundred years.

Children's games magically transcend geographical barriers for even on the remote island 'Tag', 'What's the Time Mr Wolf' and

'Doctor, Doctor' are played – the latter involving a number of children tangling together by linking hands, the 'Doctor' untangles the group without anyone releasing a held hand.

'Elastics' is usually confined to the playground, and is played by making a series of jumps in and out of a large loop of elastic.

Lingual agility is another form of childhood games, better than –

Peter Piper picked a peck of pickled pepper, or
Sister Susie stitching socks for soldiers,

are the *risqué* renderings of such modern phrases as –

I chased a bug around a tree,
I'll have his blood he knows I will.

Mairzydotes and dozydotes
And liddle lamzytivy
A kiddely tivytoo
Woodenu-oo

Sung with such frequency over the airways, was this nonsensical verse of the Second World War that is said to have so bemused Japanese Intelligence when they listened in to the wireless that it occupied the efforts of nine generals for days on end!

A prize addition to the schoolchildren's repertoire, who had the innoxious little ditty de-coded in no time:

Mares eat oats and does eat oats
And little lambs eat ivy;
A Kid'll eat ivy, too,
Wouldn't you?

Children's games and traditional nursery rhymes are played out in a realm of half-fantasy, half-reality in which they rule supreme; where code and conduct, lore and language of their making are theirs alone – a legacy to that secret world of childhood when they have left it for the next generation.

Most are national, but many are local, and expressions, like dialect, tend to be regional. Caerwent children, like many of the Welsh, call their 'safe and out of bounds' place 'Cree'. Cotswold children call for a respite by calling 'feenigs' – and these are duly respected by one's opponents.

At Apperknowle in Derbyshire the children call ox-eye daisies moonpennies – six miles away in Chesterfield they are known as pennymoons.

10 Apr. 1910 Mr Cecil Sharp visited the school this morning to listen to children's games.

Coates, Glos.

Wisborough Green School, Sussex

The end of a school day at Betwsyn Rhos in 1955

Children's games are a kind of aural antiques and we should collect and record them before they are superseded completely by the slick sophistication of the video presentation. Children are by nature great imitators and if they do not continue the traditional games of their own region we shall lose a vibrant pulse from our living heritage. Already there are some schools where children 'do not know how to play', where passive watching has taken the place of active participation, but, happily, there are still to be found little knots of children enacting the rituals of boys and girls 'out at play'. A random survey of playground and singing games produced an interesting variety, some of which are totally local to their village school.

'Hare and Hounds' – 'In the old days the boys would disappear to Dunkery for the afternoon'.

Cutcombe, Som.

'Linky' – a tig game.

Apperknowle, Derby.

'Cock-a-Rooster'
'Stoolball' – Sussex/Kent game.

Wisborough Green, Sussex

'In and out the dancing bluebells'.

Betwsyn Rhos, Clwyd

'Fair Rosa'.
'May Sat A-Sewing'.
'M.I.L.K. – Cats in Cupboard'.

Berry Pomeroy, Devon

'Tobacco'.
'Captain, Captain 1.2.3'.

Willoughby-on-the-Wolds, Notts.

'Skipping games – 'Yellow, Yellow'.
'Spinning rope game'.

Penclawdd, West Glamorgan

'Tag', 'Deno'.

Oakley Park, Powys

'Elastics'.
'Ring o' Roses'.
'French Cricket'.

Dunkirk, Kent

'Kingy' – playground game.

May Day parade with late spring daffodils at Appleby Magna

'Snot-rag' – played around the geodome.
St Katherine's, Durley, Wilts.

CUSTOMS

Come lasses and lads, get leave of your dads
And away to the Maypole hie,
For every he has got him a she,
And a fiddler's standing by.

May Day has come through the Christian calendar from the first day of Mary's Month – the month dedicated to the Virgin Mary, symbolised the crowning of the Queen of the May – and has been celebrated since the Middle Ages at Warden, famous for its pear pies long before the village became Old as a Victorian estate village. Maypole dancing lives on today at most village schools not so much as a celebration of spring rites, but within the repertoire of country dancing specified as part of the physical education training. Disciplined movements to music being a more enjoyable way of achieving the aims of regulated exercises.

Singing around the village on May Day is still done at Appleby Magna in Leicestershire and its neighbouring village of Snarston. The children of Sir John Moore School go through the village with garlands, from which they pluck blooms to give to the ladies *en route*, singing

Sing a song of May time,
Sing a song of Spring,
Flowers are in their beauty,
Birds are on the wing.

Blossom on the hedgerows,
Sunshine on the hills,
Oh! the happy May time,
All my being fills.

Chorus
May time, play time,
God has given us May time,
Thank Him for His gifts of love,
Sing a song of Spring.

The sharp-eared might catch the odd line from a teacher which *might* sound like:

May Day, May Day,
When the Dickens is pay day!

With depleted floral embellishments the children then dance around the maypole, collecting money for the old people's Christmas party.

To be May Queen is many a little girl's dearest dream. But perhaps only one in all history could claim the honour of having been crowned by the Queen of England. Aston Fence Junior and Infant School of Woodhouse Mill was celebrating its centenary when the Queen visited South Yorkshire on 12 July 1977 as part of her Silver Jubilee programme. Rotherham schools and youth organisations staged an exhibition on the playing-fields of Maltby School; Aston Fence turned up in Victorian costume and gave a display of Maypole dancing, two days before their usual Queen Day ceremony. The retiring School Queen and the Queen Elect together with their retinue lined up for the real Queen. As Her Majesty approached their stand, Alison Callan, the School's Queen Elect, held up a notice which said, 'Dear Queen Elizabeth, would you please crown me Queen of Fence School'. The Queen said, 'I'll try', and, despite carrying her flowers, she took the school-made crown and placed it on Alison's head.

The Rose Queen and ozier-gathering customs of Humberside have been replaced at New Holland School by a Festival Week.

Aston Fence School's May Queen Alison is crowned by Queen Elizabeth

Paradoxically for such a custom conscious country, tenacious to tradition and rooted in history, England's saint is nationally ignored. The village school at Clyst St George is an exception, but it does have exceptional nomenclative connections, and celebrates St George's Day in medieval style with fayres and sword dancing. An old Devon game has also been recently revived at Lady Seaward's School: Shinty was originally played with walking sticks and a wooden ball, and took its name from the players' shins which received as many if not more of the blows, so that players later wore shin pads to protect them. Today, Shinty is much less vicious and played to hockey rules, using a French-made kit; using a puck, instead of a ball, is an introduction to the game of ice hockey.

29 May 1878 (Oak Apple Day) Refused to allow boys to bring leaves into the school this morning.

Farmor's, Fairford, Glos.

The custom of wearing oak leaves, to commemorate the escape of Charles II by hiding in Boscobel Oak after the Battle of Worcester, was long-standing in schools. Those who did not sport the leaves were ridiculed and stung with nettles; this generally infiltrated into school causing disruption and litter. It was known as Shick-Shack Day in the Vale counties, where patriotic passion has manifested itself over the centuries to become a belated May Day celebration at Elmley Castle, for it was close by, at Kersoe, that the fugitive king escaped from the Roundheads due to a local man driving a hay wagon in their path.

More practical than patriotic is the reason Oak Apple Day is celebrated at Great Wishford. This is the day the schoolchildren wake up the village by banging tins and pans with the call, 'Grovely, Grovely, Grovely and all Grovely' as a signal to the villagers to reaffirm their ancient rights of collecting firewood from Grovely Wood. The charter of 1603, confirming those rights, is read during a service held in Salisbury Cathedral, some five miles away. Bonnetted women dance on the cathedral green carrying bundles of sticks as part of the festivities. Tenacious to its customs and proud of its past, the school houses a small museum of village life in its school hall.

A local version of the West Country wassailing custom was peculiar to Charlton Kings, a village straggling the wooded hill above Cheltenham. Until the outbreak of World War II schoolboys went to the 'big houses' Buff Blowing for pennies or pies, chanting some variation of

Buff blow, fare well,
God send, ere well.
Every Spring and every spray,
Apples to roast and nuts to crack,
Or a barrel of cider right to tap.
Choo-ee, choo-ee.

This is similar to the 'Thomasin' Day at Down Ampney – the village where Ralph Vaughan Williams was born and perpetuated as the hymn tune of 'Come Down, O Love Divine'.

Collecting by custom brought colour and respectability to what might, under less ceremonial circumstance, be regarded as bold begging to be accepted and expected in many regional traditions. The Cumbrian custom of tying the church gates at weddings is still carried out – much to the delight of the schoolchildren of Kirkandrews-on-Eden who scramble for the coins thrown by the bridegroom to untie the gates. Over the southern border, Lancashire lads and lassies stretch a rope across the road to get money from guests at Slaidburn weddings.

On the other side of the Pennines, Yorkshire boys put a rope across the road outside the school to collect kisses or forfeits on the Tuesday after Easter. A survival of the medieval Hocktide (Hoke Day, Hoc or Binding Tuesday) custom, it was perpetuated as Kissing Friday in the Dales, to end the week comprising Collop Monday, Pancake Tuesday, Ash Wednesday and Fritter Thursday, until at least the Fifties.

The Peak District is the region for well-dressing. Originating in pagan rites when the gods were thanked for the natural springs;

villagers left gifts at well heads to encourage them to keep the waters flowing. The votive offerings turned into exquisite works of rustic art as the simple sprays of wild flowers transformed into great scenes of some scriptural story, 'painted' with the petals of the flowers, grasses and leaves of the countryside. Well-dressing is a truly village affair and most village schools take an active part in the dressing. Tissington is famous for its beautifully dressed five wells on Ascension Day, but Litton, near Buxton, hold their well-dressing celebrations in late June.

Eyam in Derbyshire dress their wells on the last Saturday in August. Schoolchildren work side by side with pensioners and all ages in between to cover the clay puddled boards completely by the flora gathered in and around the pretty moorland village with its tragic past. Generally known as Plague Village, Eyam stands out in history for its self-sacrifice when it isolated itself as the plague struck in 1665. The 1986 dressing illustrated the story. Some 300 man, woman and child hours went into making up the mosaic of flower petals and the telling lines were picked out in hemlock seeds –

Below the hills where
  the first mourning beam
Pours all its glory on
  the graves of Eyam.

The graves of whole families wiped out by the plague dot around the village, turf mounds of the 250 who died out of an estimated population of 350.

How soon the village recovered from such decimation can only be gauged by the tablet in the church stating that a former rector of Eyam, Dr Edward Finch, bequeathed 100 l. to the school for teaching five poor children of the town and five of the out-hamlets, from land purchased in the parish of Hope between 1740 and 1750.

A further endowment was made in 1745 to 'such person as should officiate as schoolmaster at Eyam', the yearly sum of 5 l. 'for ever' to teach five poor boys and five poor girls to read and write – from the Thomas Middleton's Legacy.

The Charities and Education Commissioners Reports (1815-39) record a schoolhouse and a large school room, which were rebuilt in 1826 by voluntary contributions, the old school buildings having been sold in 1792. A public meeting was held in December 1870 to discuss building a new school to comply with the Education Act; the new school of two rooms was built by public subscription as a Church of England School and opened on 15 November 1877, under Mr and Mrs Prentis. An Infants room was added in 1894.

Monyash School is responsible each year for their Children's Well, as is Penny Acres at Holmesfield.

Well-dressing at Bisley in the Cotswolds is a fairly recent custom in

Well dressed by Eyam children

terms of hoary traditions. Inaugurated in 1863 by the Revd Thomas Keble, whose brother John was the famous poet-curate and Tractarian, after whom Keble College was founded, the ceremony of the Blessing of the picturesque Bisley Wells has become a village school tradition. It is Bisley Blue Coat School that organises the garlands of flowers on frames, enlisting help from parents and grandparents, many of whom dressed the wells in their own schooldays.

The whole village is combed to supply enough flowers in the 'between times' in which Ascension Day falls – too late for spring blossoms and too early for summer blooms. Assembling in the school playground and progressing in age order, the oldest children head the procession carrying their flowery stars, led by the vicar and the brass band. As part of the service of blessing, the schoolchildren arrange their floral letters to spell Ascension and the year. Tiny tots place their tiny posies around the wells and the ceremony is concluded with a hymn.

In true village tradition, the children are regaled with a tea, and round off the day with an evening of good old-fashioned sports such as three-legged, sack and egg-and-spoon races.

Further down the Cotswold escarpment children participate in the ancient traditions of Randwick Wap, the Cranham Feast and cheese-rolling down Cooper's Hill.

Painswick schoolchildren learn a special hymn for the celebration of Clipping Sunday in September; 'clipping' coming from the Saxon word *ycleping*, meaning embracing, and the villagers embrace their parish church by joining hands in the outdoor service. Children wear flowers in their hair and receive a coin and a Painswick bun, a large currant bun made specially by the local baker, for their lively contribution to this ancient custom.

'Obby, obbly, Onker!   My first Conker
I Tilly Ack!   My first Crack ...

The challenging cry of country boys when they find their first horse chestnut is an age-old autumn custom of childhood. Veterans of the game soak theirs in vinegar and bake them in a slow oven, before drilling a hole through the core and threading them on string or a bootlace. The conqueror – from whence the conker got its name – is the one who succeeds in splitting his opponent's nuts by striking them with his own.

The village of Haxey in Lincolnshire celebrates the Haxey Hood on Epiphany 6 January. The school closes on this day to allow the children to take part in the Junior Hood, which takes place earlier in the day than the boisterous rugger type game of medieval origin. The

Haxey Hood Game is said to date from the thirteenth century when the Lady de Mowbray lost her red hood as she rode to church. The game is played with thirteen hoods instead of a ball, to represent the thirteen villagers who found the hood. Twelve hoods are of sackcloth material stitched into a tight roll, the thirteenth is of leather. Haxey School, now housed in modern open-plan buildings, has an educational foundation dating back to 1654; and benefits from a rent of land endowment.

The Log Books of the village school in The Nooking record a 'locking out' day in February. The custom, was referred to by Dr Johnson who described Addison as a leader of a 'barring out' about 1685. At Tideswell in the Peak District the children used to carry each other to school on poles on Shrove Tuesday, rush in together and declare:

Barley, master, barley,
Barley in a spoon.
If you don't give us a holiday
We'll bar you out till noon!

In 1702 the governors of Chipping Campden Grammar School took a firm line on barring out the masters: 'if any of the Scholars be instrumental in pushing the master out of the school, they shall from henceforth be incapable of having any benefit of the said School.'

From 1708, by order of the founder, Lightmaker – nephew of Archbishop Leighton – St Giles Primary School at Horsted Keynes receives 'plumb cake' after attending church at the end of term. This West Sussex School has also established two other traditions, a Mumming play and a Boy Bishop.

Boy Bishop is an old custom held in honour of St Nicholas – Santa Claus – the patron saint of children.

CURRICULUM

An unlesson'd girl, unschool'd, unpractised:
Happy in this, she is not yet so old
But she may learn.

Shakespeare, *The Merchant of Venice*

The 'Three R's', Writing, Reading, and Arithmetic, were but beggarly elements of a dull curriculum, driven home by tedious repetition and mechanical rote, to be worked through similarly monotonous exercises. These were the fundamentals on which Robert Lowe had based his infamous 'Payment by Results' examinations. The later introduction of such subjects as History,

Geography, Agriculture and the Sciences obviously met with his disapproval, as revealed in his letter to Lord George Hamilton.

> When I was in the Education Department, as my eyes hurt me a good deal, whenever I went into the country I used to send to the National School to ask them to let me have one or two boys and girls who could read well … I found that few, if any, could really read. They got over words of three syllables, but five completely stumped them. I therefore came to the conclusion that, as regards reading, writing and arithmetic, which are three subjects which can be definitely tested, each child should either read or write a passage or do some simple sum of arithmetic; and the idiots who succeeded me have piled up on top of the three R's a mass of class and specific subjects which they propose to test in the same way.

Among some old papers found at what is now Harenc School at Foots Cray, the careful handwriting of little Ethel Billings has a maturity about it that speaks of the old copying book exercises; undated but perhaps giving some clue as to its period by the inclusion of Somme and Rheims among the spellings of 'besieged, intercept and attentive'. An earlier lesson paper is a carefully copied piece on 'duty towards my neighbour … to love honour and succour my father and mother: to honour and obey the Queen and all that are put in authority under her. To submit myself to all my governors, teachers, spiritual pastors and masters.'

Emma Morgan's beautifully written story, *A Clever Dog*, is probably a survivor from the days of the inspections on which the grant depended, as it is on official 'Practice Paper'. A sum, dated 4 September 1895 supposes a transaction between Mr Brown who traded with Thomas White of Foots Cray – and with the clue of a purchase of 156 buns at 7½d per dozen we assume Thomas White was the local baker.

Writing was often an 'extra' in the early school curriculum. Paper was too expensive to be wasted on children's work and ink needed pens. Sometimes the quills were obtained from the farmer's geese and all kinds of mixtures made some version of ink – soot and water, soot and spit, and, in Somerset, soot was mixed with cider.

Wrighting, Reading, and Navigation were the Three R's of Lady Seaward's School with its strong link with Topsham Seaport. Wrought work was an important part on the curriculum in the early days of the school as the boys were trained basically to become sailors.

It was at the village school at Clyst St George where the great Domesday Project was pioneered and the BBC used Lady Seaward's School again for a follow up of vocational training in education.

Schemes of work, set books and poems – the latter usually chosen for their moral rather than literary quality – had to be approved by

Clyst St George where the BBC Domesday Project was pioneered

Her Majesty's Inspectors. Even after a liberalising of the rigid curriculum, the general attitude can be summed up by this comment on suggestions for grammar: 'Include conjugation of verbs on a given model (a few tenses at a time can be given). This is systematic and helps to plough and harrow the brain.'

Gardening class at Farmor's School, Fairford, 1921

Cookery class at Farmor's School, Fairford, 1922. Note the 'sleeve protectors'

Buttoned-up, booted and bowler-hatted at Borthygest

As an impetus to broadening the curriculum, the newly structured county education committees relieved schools of the confines of the Revised Code in 1904 and many aimed at centring country school life on the garden, the study of Nature and the workshop. School gardens emerged from the muddy perimeters and Log Books are punctuated with references to the weather conditions affecting the time-table. In Gloucestershire alone, school gardens increased from six in 1903 to 117 by 1914.

The Gardening Class achieved 10 potatoes from one root, totalling 7 lb 1 oz – the result of one seed potato of 2 ozs and a small matchbox full of manure.

Farmor's, Fairford, Glos., 1909

Captain Oats offered to hire a garden and provide seeds and manure it if (the Head) Mr Wells would teach the boys gardening.

Besthorpe, Notts., 1915

Handicraft and domestic arts ranged across the country from woodwork to poultry-keeping, laundrywork to butter-making, but varied from county to county. As early as 1912 a special van was visiting remote Cotswold village schools, with its teacher, to give three or four weeks' intensive training in domestic science – often to a group of schools. At Besthorpe in Nottinghamshire, six girls were sent each week to Collingham in 1922 for cookery lessons; they went by carrier's cart.

When Borthygest School opened in 1880 the Headmaster complained that only a few of the children understood English. After the introduction of the Revised Code, Welsh language was not a compulsory subject under the payment by results system. However, David Thomas, the Headmaster, included it on the time-table for his school in 1892. Mr Alun Roberts has made a positive contribution to the living culture since he became Headmaster in 1975, holding evening classes for parents who wish to learn Welsh. The school itself has gained creditable honours in the Urdd National Eisteddfods over recent years, regularly visit the Urdd camps and was chosen to appear in the television programme *Hyn o Fyd*.

John Evans, Britain's oldest man, born in 1877 knew no English until he went to the village school only to find that speaking his native Welsh was a punishable offence. At least he had an education, something that had been denied his father who was sent to work at the age of five as a shepherd boy because his mother couldn't afford to feed him. The memory is still vivid over a hundred years later for John Evans recalls how he was made to stand on one leg for an hour in the corner of the classroom for talking in his native tongue.

The Welsh language was banned in state schools in the nineteenth century, even in those areas where Welsh was the first language of all

The penalty for speaking their native tongue in Welsh schools was the wearing of the 'Welsh Not' tag – punishment was meted out at the end of the day

the children. Pupils were encouraged to spy upon each other and those caught speaking Welsh at anytime in the school day were made to wear a wooden tag, branded or carved with the letters WN – meaning 'Welsh Not'. The pupil carrying it at the end of the day was duly punished.

The last great champion of Welsh independence, Owain Glyndwr, married Margaret Hanmer in Hanmer's village church – known as the Church of the Shining Mere from its elevated position above the wooded lake. The old campaigner would be duly gratified to know that the village school at Hanmer has, today, some six centuries later, a Welsh Room.

Welsh is now being taught to the Welsh as a first and second language in primary schools. Under the Athrawon Bro (Area Teachers) Welsh Service, Dyfed has employed area teachers since 1978 in schools after consultation between the headteachers and the Language Adviser. There are also Welsh language courses at camps such as the Llangrannog Urdd Camp. One area teacher is available for teaching parents of the pupils of Gartheli School in Llwyngroes village. Many school brochures are now printed in both English and Welsh.

> One point of interest in the area is the influx of English speaking children to schools that were at one time predominantly Welsh speaking. When I came here in 1966 only one out of 28 pupils came from an English speaking home. Today, the number is 17 out of 30. By the time they leave for Secondary School they will be perfectly bilingual – that is our aim, and this is true of many of the rural schools in this part of the country by now.
>
> Oswyn Williams, Betws Gwerfil Goch CP School, Clwyd, 1986

Devon was the first county to form an official 'twinning link' with a similar area on the continent, and in recent years many towns and villages in the county have formed links with towns and villages in Devon's twin area, the Department of Calvados in Normandy. The civil parish of Burrator has been twinned with Mathieu, a village eight kilometres north of Caen, since 1976. Lady Modiford's School at Walkhampton is officially linked with Ecole de Mathieu.

Educational visits are now an integral feature of the school curriculum, no longer are children confined to the four walls of their classroom – visiting and experiencing counties, countries and cultures of which their grandparents had rarely read.

SCHOOL DINNERS AND MILK

Charles Dickens once said that there was a Society for every activity, and sure enough, even school dinners – the eternal butt of schoolboys' jokes – can be traced back to Victorian philanthropic administration. The Destitute Children's Dinner Society was founded in 1864 and this was followed by other charities in other cities, including the London School Dinner Association, sponsored by the London School Board, in 1889. But these were only for the town poor and only in winter. Country poor survived by their own initiative.

Recruitment for the Boer War revealed grave malnutrition throughout the country and a Royal Commission reported on Britain's 'physical deterioration'. Arising from this the Education (Provision of Meals) Act was passed in 1906 to give local education authorities power to set up a school meals service, but limited the rate grant to 'one halfpenny in the pound over the area of the authority'.

The national crises between the two World Wars and the general depression of the 1920s extended the service to provide breakfasts as well as dinners. A new generation of undernourished children were to be aided by free or reduced cost meals, but the law (which was not free from obscurity) held that to qualify a child must be not only poor but actually suffering from malnutrition. A dietician was appointed to the Medical Branch of the Board of Education in 1938, at a time when the school meals service was extending into the rural areas. Generally, 'necessitated cases' went to 'feeding centres', and those who travelled long distances to school had 'school canteens'. The dietician's report was a depressing picture of poor quality and quantity served in unsatisfactory conditions, with the result that most authorities made an effort to improve the standards so that 'no child was too ill-fed to take advantage of his education'.

The role of school meals during the Second World War was recognised as part of the war economy and the Board of Education urged local authorities to provide them for all children at an economic rate as a matter of urgency. The Nutrition of School Children circular of 1941 states that the Government accorded the service the status of the utmost national importance in order to safeguard the health of the rising generation. 'There is the further factor that as women increasingly enter employment the children's main meal of the day may be in danger of being neglected: alternatively women will be deterred from taking up war work because of the need for attending to their children's mid-day meal and the war effort will suffer accordingly'. The government grant allowed the Board of Education to equip and staff the service and the Ministry of Food gave schools the benefit of an improved scale of allowances of rationed foods. The price of the standard 1,000 calories meal, was fixed at 5d (2p).

Where it was impossible to cook hot dinners schools were encouraged to provide an 'Oslo' meal of 2/3rd pint of milk, 3 ozs. brown bread, ¾ oz. margarine, 1½ ozs. cheese, raw vegetables and fruit,

School dinner in the hungry Forties

preferably oranges. As women replaced men on the farms and in the factories and village schools bulged with evacuees, the little sculleries and lean-to huts could not cope with such mass cooking, so many evacuated children went to 'feeding centres' or 'settlements' to relieve the families with whom they were billeted. Feeding centres were re-christened as school canteens in 1940. The importance of maintaining school canteens during the war was paramount as they were classified as emergency central points for the community.

A canteen and air-raid shelter have been built, the first additions to the school since it was founded.

Appledore, Kent, 1940

The 1943 target of providing some three million meals a day to cater for 75 per cent of school children was not realized due to delays in preparing for the Normandy invasion and the urgent deployment of funds to repairing war damage. Nevertheless, the 1944 Education Act under local authorities were required to provide meals and milk in all maintained schools 'who desired them' – extending the service to weekends and holidays where necessary – gave the scheme new impetus and legal responsibilities, and an immediate post-war programme of purpose-built dining halls and kitchens. Most village schools had to (and still do) make do with a small extension at the back for cooking, and a push-together of desks to turn a classroom into a 'dining hall'.

Social change in British eating habits is reflected in school dinner menus, even allowing for the enforced frugality of the war years. In 1942 roast mutton, potatoes and sprouts was followed by rice pudding with a dollop of jam; cheese and lentil pie, served with watercress, was accompanied by steamed bread and carrot pudding – containing a pound of raisins distributed somehow in a pudding to feed one hundred hungry youngsters. Today's school dinners offer a wide variety of dishes, such as sweet and sour pork with sauté potatoes followed by butterscotch tart piped with cream; spaghetti bolognese accompanied by yoghurt and Viennese biscuits. The great British pudding seems to have fallen out of fashion or favour.

Despite sweeping national changes towards centralized catering on a commercial basis, with school cooks never cooking because as 'catering supervisors' they supervise the ordering, costing and distribution of prepared, pre-cooked, pre-packed packs, there are still homely dinners home-baked in many small country schools.

In the simple complexity of village school life, it can be the cook not the computer that is the scholastic coadjutor. When the children of Sapperton explored the history of their village there was no programme to call up the answers to their curiosity on the old Thames and Severn Canal which runs through the valley, but there was Moira. Moira Gobey was able to tell them of a way of life long since gone because she had lived in the house on the towpath beside the bridge; an experience lengthened by the tales her grandfather had told her of the leggers who were hired at the Bricklayers Arms (now The Daneway Inn) to 'leg' the barges through the two-and-a-quarter mile tunnel by lying on their back and 'walking' along the roof. It is Moira who has enough spoons for the egg-and-spoon race, the jam-jars for the painting class, the dab of soda or splash of vinegar

Pat Pinnell, headmistress of Sapperton, worked with her pupils to produce *Village Heritage*, an award-winning book

when nettles or insects sting tiny hands, the paper bags for collecting treasures of the countryside and the pickle pot in which the first sticky buds are stuck in high windows for the little ones to witness the miracle of spring's awakening.

Across the valley at Coates, Mrs Tibbles lived through the changes wrought over her old village school, waiting on and watching over the dinner-times of the fourth generation of Tibbleses. At Bibury in the Coln Valley they still have a 1942 Ministry of Food licence to use the school as a Catering Establishment, but it was a local event for which they hoisted the Union Jack in recent years. It may not have been special in the national calendar but the entire school was celebrating – the cook's bitch had finally given birth to her pups!

Bibury is one of the many villages at which pensioners now avail themselves of the opportunity to have a school dinner, integrating a mixed-age community to the benefit of everyone as experiences widen and social exchanges sharpen.

All in all, the village school dinner has always been far better fare than that which writers recall so vividly of their meals in the early public schools. Richard Burton, the Victorian scholar-traveller, likened his Richmond School to 'a kind of Dotheboys Hall' where 'dinner began with stickjaw (pudding) and ended with meat – as badly cooked as possible, black out and blue inside ... and Saturday was a day to be feared on account of the peculiar pie which contained all the waifs and strays of the week'.

The school free milk scheme was introduced as part of the meal for necessitous children in 1924. Ten years later it was launched nationally in a co-operative by the Milk Marketing Board and the Board of Education at ½d. per one-third pint; it was free to all pupils in 1946. The scheme was subject to all kinds of administrative and practical problems until the Education Act of 1980 finally relieved local authorities of their former difficult-to-define duty relating to its provision.

Milk, like crusts and cabbage, beloved by nutritionists, is usually abhorred by children.

Mr Gunning put into operation a scheme for providing each child with a cup of hot cocoa, with milk and sugar, at mid-day. The charge is 1½d. per head per week.

Hemington, Avon, 1927

'Malted milk' was introduced into school in the Thirties to assist the milk scheme; mixers and beakers were provided free by Horlicks. The origins of the world's first dried milk for infants can be traced back, appropriately enough, to a cow, a rather fractious cow, in fact. It was a Mrs O'Leary's cow that kicked over the lamp that started the great Chicago fire in 1871. The upsurge in demand for building materials brought trade and prosperity to the Horlicks brothers, who had emigrated to America from their Forest of Dean village. Investing their fortunes in manufacturing dried 'maltings', which became a world-wide success, the Horlicks family returned to their native Gloucestershire and gave their name to 'malted milk', an important emergency food in war-time canteens and hospitals, and a tasty inducement to the children to 'take their school milk' for the good of their bones and teeth.

SCHOOL MEDICALS

Before Medical Officers of Health were introduced in 1875, the Headteacher had the sole responsibility of judging whether a child should be excluded from school on account of a potentially infectious illness. Too often it was impossible to make the diagnosis early enough, and the cramped, often damp and poor-ventilated conditions of both homes and school were the hot-beds for breeding full-scale epidemics. The Schools were not equipped to deal with even minor first-aid – at least in their own mean homes the children had the benefit of the old wives' store of cures, albeit the faith often proved more efficacious than the cure proved effective. So, it was at home that the cuts were sealed with tallow candle, cobwebs were used to staunch bleeding, and bronchial and asthmatic children were marched miles to find the road-menders so that they could be hung over the hot tar fumes!

The children of Widecombe-in-the-Moor were encouraged to drink water from the trough in which the blacksmith plunged his red-hot iron shoes to harden – on the assumption that the 'iron water' would make them strong!

28 March 1884 Dismissed the children by a quarter to twelve for the rest of the day. The men having commenced to empty closets in connection with the school at 9, and the stench in school becoming so bad that it was injurious to remain. The assistant had gone home ill through it, my throat was getting worse. The Condy's Fluid failed to remove the offensiveness.

Drayton Parslow, Bucks.

During the Midsummer Holidays the school to be cleaned, walls washed down and each room to be fumigated with sulphur candles.

Wordsley, Staffs., 1895

The Report on Physical Deterioration, which revealed serious defects in the nutrition, physique and health of the nation's children, shocked the politicians into action. Although the provision of school meals was still a voluntary scheme in most counties, and some Education Authorities had taken initial steps to arrange for District Nurses to inspect pupils as a precaution against infectious diseases, it was the Administrative Provisions Act of 1907 which made it a duty of the Authorities to set up regular and systematic medical inspections.

Infestations of the head was the first campaign and generations of schoolchildren recall the days of 'Nitty Nora on her big head hunt', squirming under the probing fingers of the District Nurse and the watching eyes of their peers queued up waiting their turn, dreading the letter home and the obnoxious-smelling lotion but, worse of all, the shame.

By 1914 the School Dentist had joined the ranks of the authorities' army looking after the education and welfare of the British schoolchild.

THE VILLAGE IN WARTIME

Some children may try your patience by wetting their beds, but do not scold or punish; as this will only make matters worse.

Information for Householders taking Evacuees, WVS leaflet

Tales of evacuated city children to quiet isolated villages would fill a book and every now and again come out for an airing as their bedding had once come out of every window every morning 'to air in the sunshine', as *The Lancet* reported on the observation that 'somewhat unexpectedly enuresis has proved to be one of the major menaces to the comfortable disposition of evacuated urban children'. Enuresis was not the only problem – although it was no doubt exacerbated by the reluctance of the 'townies' to leave their beds to trek down a dark and cold garden path to the privy beyond the gooseberry bushes as their stoic country-bred hosts had to at that time.

Lousy heads were rife and one farmer's wife was said to have run her evacuees through the sheep dip. Many a 'dirty mouth' was reportedly 'washed out with carbolic' for such profane language 'as would make a sailor blush'. Unsociable habits, ignorance of simple manners and inadequate clothing for country living with such

Evacuees preparing for a new life at school in the country

strange stories as children being 'plastered with brown paper' or sewn into their underclothes for winter were pitted against the tales of the simple peasant life of the villages with 'no chippies, the boozer a bus-ride away but no bus to get there, no "Woolies", nor no flicks, nor nothing – nothing but nothingness in the great big fields for miles'. As winter set in many returned home preferring to face bombs in a blitzed street than blizzards in a bleak countryside. But at the outset, 1st September 1939 saw the start of the greatest shift of school populations in all history when it is reckoned that some 1,300,000 children were taken by 4,000 special trains from the London area together with their teachers into the rural regions to be billeted with countryfolk and educated at the village school. The far-reaching effects of a nation at war can still be winnowed from the grain and chaff of village school life as recorded in the Log Books. Woodchurch School sifted through their Log Books, and jogged the memories of those who had lived their schooldays in the Merseyside village in two world wars, to present a school production. Probably, at no period in the school's 300 years had national events coloured its everyday life in the same way as during those troubled times. The anxiety and austerity leavened by that irrepressible schoolboy humour which has sustained generations throughout the ages, is, perhaps only appreciated by their peers.

The recollections of World War I started off with Mr Axton, who

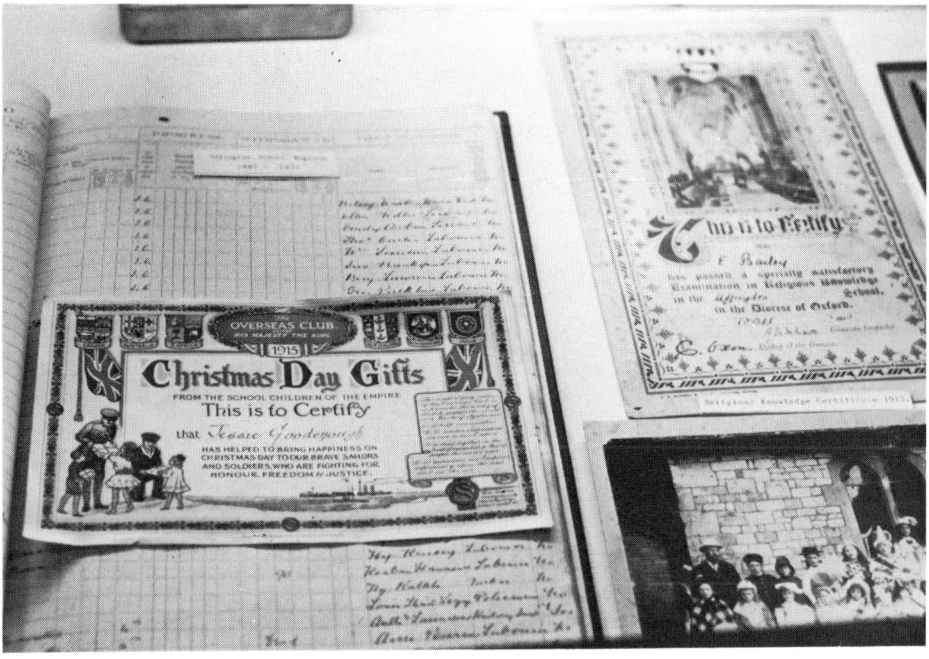

Memorabilia at Uffington

had been Headmaster since 1879 – strict, but fair, noted for keeping bees in the school garden, the boys on their toes, his Liberal politics and flaunting a warning sign of his displeasure by turning red on the back of his neck.

That year with everyone working hard for the soldiers in the war, we thought it wasn't right that some of us should be having prizes when the soldiers were suffering so badly in the war.

We collected eggs for wounded British soldiers in France – because we were a school in a country area. I mean, they wouldn't collect many eggs in the town, would they?

Then we joined in Lord Kinnaird's scheme for supplying YMCA tents for the soldiers in France. We collected eight shillings altogether. It seemed like a small fortune to us.

Two soldiers came to the school to talk to us about the war – old pupils of the school, members of the Denbigh Hussars home on leave before going back to the Front.

There you'd be in class, all quiet, working hard at your lessons, then you'd hear a squeak, or a scratching noise.

Mr Axton's neck used to get very red.

I don't know whether he was cross with us for stopping work, or cross with the mice for interrupting us – he used to throw his cane at them.

Do you remember the time the school was closed because of the mice?

And again when the boiler broke down.

Then for three weeks because of the outbreak of German measles.

I ask you, all that fighting and the school is closed because of German measles.

I remember Mr Axton reading out the King's Proclamation on the need to avoid waste. I'd heard it in Church on the Sunday as well. He seemed to go on and on just like adults do when they think they have something important to tell children. He told us not to waste any of the food we brought for our dinner at school.

The day the aeroplane landed in the fields at Landican, lots of us went to see it because we'd not seen an aeroplane before.

The next generation of Woodchurch schoolchildren experienced the effects of a war brought to what was then a small country village, and tales of evacuation and the evacuated set the scene.

Our Mums were upset over us being evacuated. I remember one child in the Infants asking why the Mummies were crying, and the teacher said that it was because they weren't going on holiday with them.

The journey seemed to last for hours – some boys from Liverpool had never been to the country before and spent the time arguing as to whether the animals in the fields they passed were sheep or cows or horses or pigs.

When we arrived we were matched in two's to the village hall. No one seemed to know what to do. A few people came in through the door and stood there pointing – 'oh, let's have him' – and 'we really want an 8-year-old girl to play with our Margaret'.

School re-opened on 1st November, 1939. The numbers had to be limited to 60 as the school shelter could only hold that number, and children returning to Birkenhead wanted to come to school here rather than in the town.

I can remember marching to the shelter. There was no panic, just a feeling of excitement as each class marched quickly across the playground. There were wooden benches and caged lights on the wall which gave off quite a good light.

We each had a tin or box in which we kept two or three comics, a book or some sweets or a toy to keep us occupied during the air raid. We used to sing 'Run Rabbit Run' and 'Ten Green Bottles', because they were songs everyone knew and they lasted a long time.

We used to try to break the record for getting into the shelter – in the end, at top organised speed the whole school could get inside in 1½ minutes.

The school had standard heavy sateen, under Defence Regulation 24, for making black-out curtains. At first, it was quite an exciting event but after a while it got quite boring.

1 July 1940 – children to attend school in the mornings only, Saturday included. Teachers take a fortnight off in turn for work – Stirrup pump practice. Very popular.

Then the war came to Woodchurch, Mr Tyson, the Headmaster recorded it in the Log Book.

19 Aug. 1940	Severe bombing during night.
30 Aug.	Air raid. Bombs dropped locally.
7 Sept.	All through the month air raids drive children into the shelter. School work has been seriously interrupted.
13 Mar. 1941	Worst raid ever. Very poor attendance. Education Office says 'Carry on'.
14 Mar.	Another night of severe bombing. Many children absent.
1 May	School building damaged after a high explosive bomb dropped by German aircraft. Four bombs in a stick dropped close to school.
2 May	School transferred to Parish Hall. Many children absent after five nights of air raids.
October 1943	School Dinners started in the Parish Hall. Yet another task for the harassed teacher – as if deciding who should get over-sized clothing coupons wasn't enough.

Isolated as some village schools are, they were not insulated from the incursions of war; within the pages of the log books are the brief statements showing how national and local events interwove: boys pinching apples, news of old boys killed on the Front Line, girls knitting socks for sailors, carol-singing for evacuee funds, a bird's nest in the chimney, flying the flag to celebrate victory in Italy.

Teachers have been asked by circular letter from the Board of Education to encourage the children to collect horse chestnuts, which may be used for certain purposes and so set free the grain that is now used for those purposes

– whatever they may be. About two bushels have already been brought to us ...

The children went to get blackberries for the last time (in connection with the Government Blackberry Scheme) this season ...

Abinger Hammer, Surrey, 1917-18

An air-raid on the night of October 2nd 1916, the children using their needlework lessons to pad splints for the wounded ... a total of 10 cwts 3 qrs 14 lbs of blackberries and 2 cwts of crab apples collected for the Government farm ...

Ardeley St Lawrence, Herts, 1914-18

Plans for badly needed extensions to Spondon House School had been accepted and contractors were preparing estimates when the outbreak of war intervened. The Derbyshire village school was already coping with fifty pupils above its maximum capacity when a classroom was taken over for a first aid room and the ARP requisitioned the wooden huts while staff dug air-raid shelters. Three forms were taught in the old Wesleyan Chapel and four more took over rooms in The Croft – the Lilleys' family house.

Staff were gradually called up with fewer replacement teachers and food became scarce just as more refugees from blitzed areas were in need of school meals, and it was nothing less than ingenuity that the 1940 Christmas dinner could boast Cornish pasty and plum pudding. Ingenuity and self help kept the canteen supplied with fresh vegetables and a yearly total of 445½ pounds of rabbit-meat as the school grounds were turned over to gardens and rabbit runs. The fuel shortage of the winters were partly relieved by the children collecting fuel from the dumps and carrying it to school. Boys helped in the distribution of ration books and raised £100 for the Prisoner of War fund while school carried on its as near normal life and functions, but it was not until the end of the war that the Headmaster 'at last felt free to enter hospital for his long overdue operation'.

The National Emergency brought evacuees to the village schools from all over the country, swelling the numbers dramatically and straining already meagre resources. In some villages it was necessary for schooling to be on a shift basis.

13 Sept. 1939 — Re-opened one week late due to outbreak of War. The children evacuated from Manchester are also in attendance and the school is being worked on the shift system – Eyam 9.00 to 12-30; Manchester 1.30 – 4.30.

There are 63 Manchester children – 18 Senior boys, 18 Senior girls, 15 Junior Mixed and 12 Infants.

By the end of October full-time education was resumed with the

Eyam School, Derbyshire

Manchester Infants and Juniors absorbed into the Eyam classes and the Manchester Seniors being accommodated in the Rectory Room.

In December 1940 the School was closed when it was used as an evacuation centre following the raids on Sheffield.

Eyam, Derby.

18 Sept. 1939 Re-opened school with 66 of our own children and 45, plus 5 Infants, London children, also their Master, Mr Brown.
Furniture at the moment to be supplemented by trestle tables and chairs from Turner's Tower Clubroom.

Hemington, Som.

Schools provided the necessary labour on country farms from which the menfolk had been taken to serve on the Front. In the Isle of Ely, the Education Committee decided that 'owing to the serious scarcity of labour they will raise no objection to boys and girls of 12 years of age and over being absent from school between September 27 and November 17 to assist in agriculture operations'.

However, the quiet out-of-the-way places in the countryside were often no safer than the towns and cities.

6 Sept. 1940	Air Raid warning 8.55. Guns and Bombs heard. Children encouraged to sing loudly. Perfect behaviour. All clear 10.5.
19 Nov. 1943	An officer called to see if the school might be used for sleeping men on manoeuvres. Premission was granted.
	Abinger Hammer, Surrey
15 Aug.	Following intensive Air Raids and bombing in this district last night the registers were not marked until 10 a.m.
	Netherton C. of E. School, Worcs.
29 Aug. 1940	Attendance for the past week has been poor. This is due to the Air Raid Warnings each night, which have generally lasted from 10 p.m. until 4 or 5 a.m.
17 Feb. 1941	Fire-watching will be carried out in this area. The School will be used as a centre for John Street, Brook Street, Camp Hill and Bridge Street.
8 May 1945	This was official Victory in Europe Day. Service of Thanksgiving with other Wordsley Schools in Parish Church.
	The Brook School, Wordsley, Staffs.

The trivial and the tragic link together in the fabric of village school life.

A policeman called to complain about boys throwing stones ... eldest boys allowed to go and see potatoes being sprayed by the County Council ...

Blitz in the country. Little Melton School following a bombing

boys have football every fine day and their standard of play is improving … Request for Standard 3 to 5 to collect blackberries … village stunned by the news of the loss of three of its men …

Ysgol Borthygest, Gwynedd, 1918

John Travers Cornwall, boy seaman and former pupil, awarded the Victoria Cross at the Battle of Jutland 1916.

Dunkirk, Kent

The village school itself did not escape the vicissitudes of war. Little Melton in Norfolk lost its Victorian school in a bombing raid at 2 a.m. on 4 May 1943. It was the only site in the area to be destroyed. The Headmistress, Mrs Barbara Buckton, and her little son David were asleep in the adjoining schoolhouse when the bomb hit the school. The village had a temporary building for 31 years until a new school was built on a different site.

TREATS AND FUND-RAISING

I have had playmates, I have had companions,
In my days of childhood, in my joyful school-days.

Charles Lamb

20 June 1890 Picnic at Roche Abbey, the chapel children absent.

Laughton-en-le-Morthen, W. Yorks

School outings became more venturesome in the Thirties and often involved the whole village. This is the Kempsford to Southsea outing

The only outing we had was in a horse-drawn brake to Habberley Valley. We paid a halfpenny a week for a whole year. We took our own food, with a bottle of water. We walked up hills and helped to push the brake to give the horse a rest. The weather was no respecter of persons and we often got soaking wet. Yet we enjoyed every minute of what was, to us, a great adventure.

Cliff Willetts, Two Gates Ragged School, Worcs., 1909

Fund-raising has been part of school life for many years, from the early attempts to balance the School Manager's accounts to providing the extras which the Education Authorities can not or will not provide. But probably no other institutional field works harder to assist so many different needs, local, national and international, than the village school.

1942	A Social was held for the School wireless fund.
	Hemington, Som.
1948	A Concert was held in the School to entertain the Scouts who had lost their main tent during a storm.
1940	Whist Drive – to buy wool for the soldiers.
	Ysgol Morfa Bychan, Gwynedd

The suffering of war horses in Europe in the Great War reached the hearts of thousands of schoolchildren up and down the country, so much so that the Blue Cross – incorporating Our Dumb Friends' League – had its own Children's Branch, membership for which was 1d a year.

31 Oct. 1967	There was a collection of £20 8s. 6d. to the Aberfan School Disaster Fund.
	Ysgol Borthygest, Gwynedd

MEMORABILIA

Where once we dwelt our name is heard no more,
Children not thine have trod my nursery floor;
And where the gard'ner Robin, day by day,
Drew me to school along the public way,
Delighted with my bauble coach, and wrapt
In scarlet mantle warm, and velvet capt,
'Tis now become a history little known.

William Cowper

Memorabilia of school days past tend to be kept in village schools more so than in their larger town counterparts. Tangible links with the times as they changed: an old ink bottle, a bent cane, a cracked commemorative mug, yellowed certificates, cross-nibbed pens and ink-stained time-tables, and half-finished samplers jostle for space with faded photographs of today's parents and grandparents caught

Assembly accompanied by the harmonium at Lechlade at the turn of the century

forever in their childhood.

Sapperton School in the Cotswolds keeps a school treasure chest and pops everything into it which records the life of the village as well as the school. From their store they found vital pieces of the village jigsaw around which they built up their award-winning book *Village Heritage*. Many schools have something written on their history – from an introductory paragraph in the school brochure to a full-size published book; by 1966 some 2,000 histories of Old Schools had been catalogued. Others like Studham in Bedfordshire keep a scrapbook of pupils' work on their village over the years.

Wisborough Green School has the wooden yoke on which the pails of water were fetched before the delightful Sussex village was put on 'the Mains' in the Thirties.

Surrey's Horsell First has the original plans and specifications of its School, built in 1851.

Inkwells, old ink, and an abacus are retained at Timberscombe Ceva First School, among with the memories of Lance Percival being evacuated to and Anna Ford leaving her bike at, the old school, founded in 1714, in a beautiful setting on the edge of Dartmoor.

A log book of Naseby's Victorian School in Northamptonshire contains the Queen Mother's signature. The trowel from the stone laying ceremony in May 1842 is kept at Yorkshire's Woolley C. of E. School, built by public subscription – replacing an earlier seventeenth-century school across the road. Among its other Victorian memorabilia is a needlework sampler of 1826.

Lessons in humility and piety were stitched by little Mary Britain into her sampler along with her name, Berkswell School, and the date – 1849.

Be gracious to Thy servant, Lord,
Do Thou my life defend,
That I according to Thy word
My future time may spend.

Edged with grape hyacinths and pansies, with a butterfly, a small bird on a twig, and finished with a floral border, it is a charming piece of work.

Within the circumference of a leather collar, a memento retained at Berkhamsted School, is the enigmatic story of Peter, the Wild Boy. Brought to England by George I, Peter was found to be completely unteachable and spent his time at Haxter's End Farm – and later found a place in two of Dickens' novels.

Future historians will have the interesting task of unsealing the time capsule which the children of Ann Cam School filled with small items reflecting aspects of 1985. It was cemented into the wall of the Parish Church to mark Dymock's 900th anniversary – to be opened in the year 2085. It was on this village post office that the great daffodil trade centred between the wars, and the Dymock Poets

Pensive in hand-me-downs at Hatherop in the 1900s

The school bell at Kempsford has its own little wooden roof

despatched their 'New Numbers' to the four corners of the world.

The village school itself is a memorial in Hatherop. Built in 1856 by A. G. Ponsonby in memory of his father, Lord de Mauley who rebuilt the church and remodelled Hatherop Castle where Charles I once held court (now a private girls' school).

Remembrance is monumental high above the Welsh valley where a whole generation was lost on 21 October 1966, when a coal tip engulfed Pantglas village school. The loss of a school full of 116 children and 28 adults stunned the world; Aberfan will become immemorial. A Garden of Remembrance covers the site of the lost school.

The bell has a special place in the hubbub of school life. Boscastle's School bell is distinctive and is rung, as used to be customary throughout the country, to call pupils to school. The lovely old building is in an attractive Valency Valley village some half mile from the harbour – the only shelter for many storm-swept miles of Cornwall's northern coastline – and the school bell is the warning for the village in any crisis.

Bells are linked with the past of Clyst St George where the Revd Ellacombe became famous for the single-handed bell ringing system. But it is the School bell which holds a daring and dramatic tale in its toll, for it was retrieved by the British Navy off the coast of southern

A new site for the old bell at Fairford Infant School

Spain. Assumed to be a Catholic call bell, it was given to the village fire brigade who, in turn, presented it to Lady Seaward's School when it was built.

5 *Villages Old, New and Isolated*

LOST AND NEW VILLAGES

Sweet smiling village, loveliest of the lawn,
Thy sports are fled, and all thy charms withdrawn,
Amidst thy bowers the tyrant's hand is seen ...

Oliver Goldsmith

Some regional differences and national similarities in village schools must be attributed to the foundation of the village itself, as a nucleated community. As we have seen earlier, most villages pre-empted State decreed education by local initiative and benefaction. It follows, therefore, that among Britain's 'lost' villages there have been many schools lost with them.

The causes of their demise are complex and diverse. Leaping across the pages of history on which William the Conqueror wrote the first chapter of subjugation, when not only the north was harried, the whole of the British Isles suffered over the centuries at the hands of the royal and religious, the noble and ignoble as they pillaged and sacked, evacuated and emparked the villages in their path. The ravages wreaked by successive monarchs were matched unworthily by land-hungry monks like the Cistercians, who laid waste whole settlements to secure seclusion for their monasteries, and pasture for their vast flocks to finance them. In one case, Sempringтon in Lincolnshire disappeared as a village because all the villagers, men, women, and children, entered the monastery.

The scourge of the Black Death took its terrible toll over 300 years and many villages died with their populace. In a number of instances the village was dismantled and rebuilt a few fields away in an effort to isolate the survivors from the plague-ridden site. The resultant labour shortage coinciding with the expansion of the wool industry dealt another devastating blow on yet more villages as they were swept away to become vast sheepwalks into Tudor times. Such was the scale of depopulation and destruction that Henry VII passed an Act against the pulling down of villages, in which he decried 'the service of God prohanced' – and this often accounts for ancient churches left isolated among the fields.

The greed of the late medieval graziers paled beside the avarice of the Stuart and Georgian aristocracy. Scores of old manorial villages were razed in the landscaping of grandiose mansions set in acres of private parkland as landowners strove for both seclusion and status. Old Newnham in Oxfordshire, which was levelled by Lord Harcourt and rebuilt by 'the tyrant's hand' as Nuneham Courteney a mile away, beyond the vista from his new mansion, is favoured by scholars as Goldsmith's Auburn – although dozens of similarly emparked villages contend the title. What is of interest is that the village school features in Goldsmith's *Deserted Village* published in 1770, so wherever contemporaries, such as Crabbe – who thought the poem sentimentalised fiction – or students of economic and social history, who draw different conclusions from the piece, actually site the village, the school from which 'the playful children' were 'just let loose' is established:

There is his noisy mansion, skill'd to rule,
The village master taught his little school.

A number of near-deserted villages, particularly in Northumberland and Nottinghamshire, have been repopulated and changed their character as colliery villages. Among the townships which have been reduced to villages by size and status over the centuries is Dorchester in Oxfordshire. Within the Abbey churchyard is a gabled building, contemporary with the Abbey's famous Jesse window, the village grammar school in Elizabethan times – now the village museum. Among its interesting exhibits is a facsimile of the first page of the School Register of 1653, and the original pen and pencil drawers. The village still retains its school, housed now in modern buildings. The old girls' and boys' schools, designed by Sir Gilbert Scott last century while he was working on the ancient Abbey, have been converted; the girls' to a private house, the boys' to the Village Hall.

Down-river Thames villages on the other hand have generally outgrown their rural roots so the definition of which can still be identified as villages becomes even more tenuous. Barnes has kept faith with the village tradition despite being officially a south-west district of London. An urban village, more than a country one, needs perceptible boundaries to mark it off from the city to which it also belongs. Topographically, Barnes has a sense of separateness that is conducive to what is really the essence of village life: embraced by the Thames as it makes its dramatic arc over the north of the parish with the Common on the southern boundary, it is difficult to leave Barnes without being aware that you are doing so. A parish church, consecrated in 1215, a pond and schools on the Green makes this a village in every sense.

The Green School, founded in 1775 for sixteen pupils, was built on the site of the old bowling green and was the only National School in Barnes until 1868. From 1883 three more schools opened: Westfields, built for infants only in 1903, is the only one left doing, *mutatis mutandis*, the same job on the original site.

It is beyond the scope of this book to search out all lost and new villages and examine the causes for their loss, or being. However, a cursory look at the establishment of the village often reflects to some degree in its school.

Estate villages are identifiable mainly by their uniformity of architectural style but other newly-built villages are not emparked in the true sense, but rebuilt as 'model' villages, such as Great Tew in Oxfordshire whose farm-workers' cottages were designed with standard half-acre gardens to be equally divided between ground for the pig and the growing of vegetables. The gabled Victorian school, often mistaken for the church, across the leafy green completes an idyllic village scene.

The forces of man and nature, sometimes individually, often combined, have destroyed villages completely even in this century. Hallsands in Devon, once a busy fishing village, was swept away in 1917 as a result of erosion by excessive quarrying of its shingle beach to provide building material for Devonport Docks.

Lancashire lost Dale Head Village when it was flooded to form Stocks Reservoir, the schoolchildren were transferred to Brennand's School in Slaidburn, in the 1930s. Endowed by John Brenand in 1717, the elegant two-storey building was originally the grammar school of this greystone village nestled in a fold of the moors below the ancient Forest of Bowland.

Half of old Rivington, to the south-west, lies below yet another reservoir, created in mid-Victorian times to provide water for Liverpool, which accounts for the long causeway approach to the remainder of this enchanting village. Happily, the old village school escaped a watery grave, sited slightly downhill from the church the present early eighteenth-century primary school was rebuilt from a grammar school founded in 1656 which was destroyed by fire. A stone post in the playground served earlier generations as a hitching post for their ponies as they rode into the old school from the outlying homesteads. The school is set on the edge of Lever Park in the National Park Area.

Salisbury Plain lost Imber and the Dorset Coast lost Tyneham to the Ministry of Defence as military training zones. Imber, home to various peoples for some 3,000 years, was an isolated village on the Wiltshire chalk downs close to the ancient Ridgeway. The small independent community, self-sufficient and living mainly from sheep-farming had two village schools: one for church children, the other for the chapel children, both for about forty pupils. In the 1830s, Imber Court became a Classical, Commercial and Mathematical Academy for young gentlemen; it was there, quartered at the Court, where the Great War soldiers first settled.

The large tracts of open downland as a training area had earlier attracted the attention of Prince Albert; the First World War brought the artillery range to Chapperton Down and as activities increased the villagers were only allowed out of Imber three times a week to shop for food. In 1932 the War Office bought the village except for the lands under the church authority, the chapel, the pub and the school. A thousand-yard safety area surrounded the village which remained inhabited until 1943, when a week before Christmas it was finally evacuated. Shell-shocked and ravaged by time, little remains of old Imber, except the church where an annual service, usually in early September, is held. The road through the village is open on certain Bank Holiday weekends, but the public are not allowed to wander at will.

Tyneham village also ceased to be in December 1943. Some 225 villagers and 102 separate properties, including the village school, were evacuated to release 7,300 acres for gunnery range facilities at Lulworth. 'We have given up our homes, where we have lived for generations, to help with the war and to keep men free. We shall return one day ...' the villagers wrote on the door of St Mary's Church. But they never returned – except as visitors to gaze at the ruins which were once their homes on a curve of Dorset's coastline – a gaunt and gallant testimony to communal sacrifice. The deserted village and the coastal path/range walks are now open to the public most weekends, Bank Holidays and during school holidays. The past has been gathered together in permanent exhibitions in the former church and the old schoolhouse.

The Northumbrian village of Ford was rebuilt altruistically by the Marchioness of Waterford in 1859 as a memorial to her husband who died in a riding accident. She restored the ancient square built fortress where James IV of Scotland slept before his death on Flodden Field, but it was at the village school she put her personal touch. A talented painter of the Pre-Raphaelite School, she decorated a room with water-colour frescoes of biblical scenes. The old school is now called Lady Waterford's Hall.

The school building at Sledmere in East Yorkshire is still owned by the Sykes family, local educational philanthropists who created what has been described as a 'superb' estate village. Royal and famous visitors to Sledmere House, set in its beautiful 'Capability' Brown parkland, have been encouraged to visit the Victorian Gothic school which Sir John Betjeman thought 'interesting and worthy of preser-

'Deliciously pseudo' is how Sir John Betjeman described the village school at Sledmere

vation'. The close ties with 'The House' and the influence of 'The Family' over the school are revealed in the Log Books.

The village school at Garton-on-the-Wolds is another Sykes family foundation. An example of early Victorian 'open-plan' arrangement, Garton School has served as village hall and evening class centre for many years. A recent extension predicts an equally busy future.

Old Warden estate village in Bedfordshire owes most of its creation to the Ongleys and the Shuttleworths. The village school, opened in 1875, closed its doors for the last time in 1986 – probably the only one to do so voluntarily.

The future of the school at Ardington, now assigned to Oxfordshire, was a major consideration when a new owner took over Lord Wantage's old estate village. A hundred years ago the village was employed by the estate. Ten years ago its population was halved as the estate decreased its holdings. To counter the threat of becoming a commuters' dormitory, the estate opened up many of its redundant buildings to attract small rural industries, bringing life, work and families to the village – and children to the school.

Victorian trade and industry created settlements around them, which in turn founded village schools for their workers' children. The school at Wookey Hole in Somerset was built by the mill for the local children in 1872. A hundred years later the school achieved its highest number with 130 on roll, but the following decade has seen the numbers fall drastically to twenty.

A village school at New Holland was in existence some thirty years before the village developed with the coming of the railway to it around 1890. A terminus for rail and ferry traffic, New Holland got its name from the early days when Dutch gin was smuggled into the Barrow-on-Humber village. The ferry service finished when the Humber bridge was opened in 1981, but the school keeps an old anchor as a reminder of the close ties with the sea. Closer ties between early religious foundations have now been sealed. In the Sixties the Infant School and Junior School amalgamated but remained in their respective school buildings: one Church of England; the other, Methodist. In 1983 the Edwardian style Infant School was extended and modernised, in 1985 a new hall and classrooms were added for the juniors, and the old Victorian building was demolished. The school is now known as New Holland C of E and Methodist. Post-war industries have also created new communities.

The old Northumbrian village of Byrness schooled twelve poor children free in 1793, when the curate was paid to teach them in the church. The opening of a road from Otterburn, nine miles down the valley, over the Carter Bar to Scotland, plus the opening of small collieries in the neighbourhood increased the population and by 1872 a school for 25 children was staffed by a full-time teacher. After two decades of infrequent attendance, poor teaching, severe weather, lack of funds, and three warnings, the school was closed, in 1895, as being inefficient.

The construction of a new reservoir brought workers with their families to the area and the school was revived and enlarged to accommodate seventy pupils; but, with the reservoir built and collieries closed, work ceased, families drifted away and the school closed in 1937 when only eight pupils were left on the register. For the next twenty-five years Byrness children had to travel down the valley to Rochester and later to Otterburn.

The new village at Byrness built on the edge of the Redesdale Forest was planned to be the largest concentration of population in Upper Redesdale therefore required a school. Designed to be erected in stages to meet increased numbers, Byrness Village School opened in 1956 for forty pupils; stage two in 1961 accommodated sixty, the final design in keeping with the village.

Mechanization eventually reduced the labour force and now only 300 men are permanently employed in the forest which gave rise to the establishment of the forestry villages. Byrness village never fully expanded as expected, due to cut-backs, but the school built to cater for the forestry workers' children is still open, with barely a dozen pupils, drawn from the village itself and the farms further up the valley. It also serves the community, as hundreds of other village schools do up and down the country, as a community centre for the local playgroup and youth club.

St Katharine's School in Savernake Forest is a school without a village. It was built in 1879 to educate children of the employees at Tottenham House estate; there are now twenty-four primary-age pupils on roll.

CHARTIST SETTLEMENTS

See there the School, where no false doctrines cloy,
But wisdom teaches duty to enjoy,
Nor clothes religion in a harlot's dress,
How rich to dazzle! but how poor to bless!

Ernest Jones, Chartist song

The most historically interesting of the new villages are not strictly villages in the same sense as a nucleated community established around church and manor, but the Chartist estates of smallholdings of such uniformity of pattern and architectural utility that they stand today as living relics of England's most famous revolutionary plan for land reform – a collective memorial of five estates, still housing over 200 families, to Feargus O'Connor, the resolute, radical reformer who founded the movement in 1845.

Neither church nor manor featured in the promised land of Chartism, although O'Connor was of strong Irish Protestant faith and found the Scriptures an easy and acceptable source to analogise when he needed to inject yet more colour in his vehement orations. The idealism which he offered to the working-class shareholders was freedom from hereditary bondage when – if they were fortunate to win tenure of a cottage in his great land lottery – they would live in 'the castle of the freeman, instead of the den of the slave'.

It was the school which O'Connor made the institution common to each estate. By doing so, within his Utopian communities there lay – as he claimed to the 'out of the way county of Devon, the land of Parsons, sour cyder, and low wages' – the means to dispense with educational aid, *inter alia* numerous other social disorders. The Devon serfs gave him a rapturous ovation, did justice to his tea-party then returned to their work for parson and feudal lord, to their cider and the security of regular, albeit low, wages; the landowners offered as their only suggestion for an estate, an isolated patch of unreclaimed land three miles up a rugged hillside. O'Connor had enough obstacles to surmount without tackling topographical problems.

It was in Hertfordshire that O'Connor built his first estate. Some two miles from Rickmansworth and fifteen from London, Heronsgate became O'Connorville in the euphoria of its opening to the public who converged in a great convoy of horse-drawn omnibuses, stage coaches, gigs, waggonettes and fly on the model village to gaze in wonder at the neat villas, spacious holdings and the school – two schoolrooms, each 24ft long, one for the boys and one for the girls, with the schoolhouse in the middle. Each house had been fitted up with 'a neat and elegant library' (as O'Connor euphemistically called the bookshelves) to show that 'the mind has not been forgotten'.

May Day 1847 welcomed the first allottees with glorious sunshine, lively band music and well-wishers; church bells rang to celebrate the possession of labour's first estate, and liberal newspapers published stirring poems as the families of fortune settled in to Paradise Number One.

Another excursion brought visitors to the cherryfield country to see how the new living had so drastically improved their health and lot in a mere three weeks. The schoolroom, decorated with greenery, accommodated the envious townsfolk who sat down to a wholesome repast of meats, pies and salads, while O'Connor pointed out the salient differences between self-sufficiency on a settlement and slavery in the 'rattle-box' and factory. The opening of the school generated the most interest: although it was eighteen months before a schoolmaster was appointed. Funds for the school clock were raised by a public soirée, but the schoolmaster was expected to pay £500 for the schoolhouse. A Mr M. D. Graves was appointed from many applicants and he immediately changed the name to O'Connorville College, advertising his curriculum and fees in the *Northern Star* as an agricultural, horticultural and model farm school, with general education, for 16 guineas per annum, with stationery extra. The children of grocers and cheese-mongers would be boarded and educated, and goods in lieu of cash would be accepted. There is no mention of the fees to be paid by the local village pupils.

The school opened in July 1848; at the end of the month the legalities of the National Land Company (as the Chartist scheme was then registered) were brought by the Select Committee for a reading in the House of Commons. The school lasted less than a decade; by 1857 the estate had been auctioned and the school converted to a private house. Feargus O'Connor had died two years previously and with him his didactic creed; 'religious discussion' found a welcome at old Heronsgate and a new school and chapel were built near the entrance.

Arches and roundels reflect an ecclesiastical influence at Redmarley in 1860

Lowbands estate in Worcestershire's fruit-filled vale was also purchased in 1846, again it was in an isolated situation. O'Connor moved into the existing farmhouse with Rebecca – his cow, famed for her summer yield of twenty-eight quarts a day – and reached the heart of the town's starved workers by promising that at Lowbands, by 'blessed change operated by democracy' the schoolhouse was rising in the place of the 'bastille' (workhouse) on the confines of the village to receive them …

– and the mother, instead of sending her children to the mill, there to brutalise the mind and waste the young form, sees them go to school with a light heart, to brighten that intellect which God gives equally to all!

The handsomely built schoolhouse, with its octagonal slated roof, and lozenge-shaped windows looking out to the Malverns, was pressed into service on Open Day – initially for serving coffee for the expected 500 visitors, then, after the neighbouring villagers of Redmarley had agreed that Lowbands crops were bigger and better than their own, for the Land Conference to convene their meeting. O'Connor, his ruddy cheeks clashing with his ginger hair, put the question to the assembly, 'when had the Whigs built schools like this one to teach them?'.

Lowbands School opened on 10 July 1848 to children and any adult who could afford to pay the master, a Mr O'Brien. Instruction was offered in English Language, science, philosophy within a broad ranging syllabus which also paid close attention to moral education. Extra-curricular activities centred on his belief that music was an incentive to scholastic progress and lessons were offered, out of school hours, in the cornopheon, ophicleide, flageolet and serpent as well as a range of other wind and string instruments. Tuition and learning must have been exceptional as, in a mere six weeks, a brass band had been formed and proved proficient enough to play 'enlivening airs' at the anniversary celebrations. Schoolmaster O'Brien, a fellow Irishman, prompted his own children to lead the Chartist song declaring allegiance to O'Connor and his ideals, and the community danced and sang until dawn rose above the Malvern hills.

A month later, O'Brien was conducting the parents of his pupils to sing a different tune when the rent was due. O'Brien rallied them against demagogue; repercussions were swift and public opinion was divided. Some saw the allottees as deluded innocents reduced to ruined paupers; others despised them as disgruntled dissipated idlers. Enquiries and surveys led to eventual collapse of the settlement as an independent community and within three years of its opening,

Lowbands were generally accepted into the parish of Redmarley.

The big schoolroom which still held the echoes of young children struggling with such advanced subjects as conic section chemistry, became the workroom for gloveresses as mothers turned their back on Chartist allotments and looked to Dent's glove factory at Worcester for their daily bread. A new school was intended but never materialised and, as at Heronsgate, religion found its way to Lowbands and a Bible Christian chapel was built soon after O'Connor's death.

The freestone quarryland of the Windrush Valley in Oxfordshire was the third estate to be settled, and the schoolhouse was well under construction within eight months of the land purchase. The new estate became Charterville. It had its own post office and all seemed prosperous until the rents were due. Within three years of its purchase Charterville was advertised for sale, and by 1852 all connections with the Chartist Land Company had been severed.

Minster Lovell built its own school in 1872 down on the lower ground in the village and of its 120 children those from the old allotments, as they were called, attended.

By 1889 the estate became known as 'little Evesham', from its development in market gardening. Although a part of Minster Lovell parish for well over a century, the old estate appears on the OS maps as Charterville Allotments and except for the loss of its bell turret, the schoolhouse remains architecturally the same as when it was built in 1848, differing in style from the schools on the other Chartist estates by having triple porches along its front.

Snigs End, bought by O'Connor in 1847, straddled two parishes: Staunton and Corse, where Gloucestershire loses its Cotswold identity to the lands of the Severn and the Welsh Marches.

The school, true to pattern, was priority on the list of buildings; this seems to be more for the sake of having one public building to house the meetings and social gatherings than for pure educational purposes.

A schoolmaster had arrived from Leicester early on, but he was only interested in buying the old farmhouse and threatened O'Connor with a hatchet when he found some of the estate already mortgaged, but the strong Irishman floored him first. It appears that the schoolmaster successfully bought the farmhouse as he was offering refreshments at his 'cyder vaults' to the visitors and prospective allottees when they arrived to gaze in awe at Snigs End Paradise.

The Chartist chapter closed on Snigs End, punctuated with the dissent and disillusion of the other estates. The schoolhouse, with it two acres, was auctioned in 1857 as a result of the Winding Up Acts of The National Land Company in 1848-49, and was held by the Staunton parish until the village school was built at nearby Corse in

The Chartist school at Snigs End. Now the Prince of Wales public house, it has barely altered externally

the early 1870s. The schoolhouse with its schoolrooms winging out each side became a public house.

The incorrigible land-hungry O'Connor bought Great Dodford in Worcestershire his fifth estate before Snigs End had its first harvest. It went under the auctioneer's hammer on 15 April 1850.

The estate villages stand today, secluded patches of our national heritage, their schools converted into dwellings and the settlements themselves integrated into the older established neighbouring villages. Only a name on an old map and the dusty records of the incredible company scheme hold the secret of those long-forgotten schools.

ISLAND VILLAGES

Islands of the British Isles have retained their identity even within the conformity of English laws, so any differences in their village schools are imposed by geographical and topographical conditions.

The Isle of Wight is England in miniature, and is actually a county in its own right dotted with a number of villages.

It is interesting to note that the depopulation of the island in the Middle Ages was considered a potential threat to the defence of the realm and was the subject of an Act in 1488 which preceded intervention by the Crown on mainland Britain's plight.

The Isle of Wight is a vastly different place today, but despite its image as a holiday island its village schools are the throbbing pulse of their own communities. It is in the small schools that the WI, the floral art club, the Cubs and Scouts, Brownies, the church fête committees and public bodies meet and carry out their business.

Godshill is a picture-book village of pretty thatched cottages with an interesting legend surrounding the origins of its grey stone church. The foundation of its education is much more factual and dates back to 1615 with an endowment from Lady Ann Worsley of Appuldurcombe. The present village school, a listed Regency-style building, was erected by Lord Yarborough, and is very much a focus of village life. The pupils in their attractive purple and lilac, white and grey uniform add distinctive colour to the country dancing which they perform at the local pub and Carisbroke Castle. Picturesque Godshill adorns calendars and chocolate boxes and its school atlas!

Chale Primary School is situated near the infamous shipwrecking and smuggling area of the Blackgang Chine.

Whippingham School, near East Cowes, has the distinction of being designed by the Prince Consort and connections with Osborne House.

Lundy celebrating Queen Victoria's Diamond Jubilee in 1897 with a picnic on the west side of the island

The tiny island of Lundy is a village in the Bristol Channel. It appears as little more than a large granite rock battered by white-crested Atlantic rollers when viewed from North Devon or South Wales, and it is true that you can walk round and across it both ways at a leisurely pace in a day. In this remote area of three miles long by a mere half mile wide, the need for 'schooling' was met by the initiative of the Revd Hudson Grosett Heaven who owned the island from 1883 until his death in 1911.

Although ordained, Revd Heaven never held a parish so became curate in charge of his own island, and as the only 'educated' man on it he assumed the role of schoolmaster. The Census of 1881 gives the total population as 31 males and 30 females, of which 7 boys and 8 girls were under the age of 10. Lessons in reading, writing and scripture classes were carried out in various houses until he built a schoolroom in 1886.

Compared with attractive stone-built Victorian schools on the mainland, Lundy School was of corrugated iron. But then, so was the little steepled church behind it. The one-room schoolroom measured 19½ feet by 11½, with walls of 6½ feet rising to a pitched roof of 10 feet. Steps led to the central door. A window each side of the door and a single window in each side admitted little daylight; the windowless back abutted on to a stone wall. But what the small school lacked in architectural style it made up for by the service it rendered to the islanders: affording day school to the children and, according to references in the Revd Heaven's diaries, many a 'school tonight' for the farmworkers and lighthouse keepers until the First World War, when Lundy was almost completely evacuated.

The corrugated iron church was demolished in 1897, but the schoolroom continued to serve as the village hall until it was renovated and extended in the 1960s to become a holiday cottage

Lundy Island School, 1965

when the National Trust bought the island and leased it to the Landmark Trust.

Foulness Island is only an island in-so-far as it is an area cut off from mainland Essex by tributaries to the North Sea. It is in fact a mudflat, but even here the village school was founded in the 1870s and survives today, albeit with barely a dozen children on roll. As a Ministry of Defence area – strongly favoured for London's third airport, Foulness has none of the tourist attractions of the other British isles, quite the reverse – as visitors have to be sponsored before they can obtain a pass to the island.

England's northernmost island on the other hand derives a high proportion of its livelihood from tourism. Holy Island, the ancient Lindisfarne, cradle of Christianity, supports five hotels – as many as there are pupils on roll at its old school. With a population of less than two hundred, there are relatively few school-age children on the island which lives by farming and lobster, crab and salmon fishing. Linked to Northumbria by a causeway, Holy Island is totally dependent on tidal conditions and schoolchildren over the age of nine board at school on the mainland during the week.

The Isles of Scilly were separated from the south-west tip of England 300,000 years before folklore severed them from the mainland. The divine retribution which legend meted out on the traitor Mordred and his army for slaying King Arthur was cataclysmic, for in drowning them the Atlantic waters also submerged the beauteous forest country threaded with sparkling streams, locked into historical fiction as the lost land of Lyonnesse, immortalised by Tennyson.

Of some hundred or more 'sun isles' and islets, from which the name Sulli has come through the centuries as Scilly, only five are inhabited today: St Mary's, the largest is but three miles by two; Tresco, famous for its Abbey gardens; St Agnes, the insular most south-westerly community of the British Isles; Bryher, the smallest, hilly, rugged and worked by farmers and fishermen, and St Martin's, the first two-mile narrow ridge of land to be seen when approached from mainland Britain.

For some fourteen centuries since Christian hermits first settled on the Scilly Isles their lease had been granted to a monastic order, then as a gift to the Black Prince and from 1337 to the Duchy of Cornwall. The value of the lease in 1306 was reckoned at a yearly rent of 6s 8d (33½p) or 300 puffins. Since their formation in 1985, the Isles of Scilly Environmental Trust has negotiated the lease of all the uninhabited islands and untenanted land of St Mary's, St Martin's. St Agnes and Bryher for ninety-nine years for the annual rental of one daffodil!

The lease on Tresco was not relinquished and is held by the Dorrien Smith family, descendants of Augustus Smith who obtained the lease of all the islands from the Crown in 1834. It was to the energy and foresight of this Hertfordshire squire that the prosperity and development of the Scilly Isles are due.

Educating the Scillonians was Augustus Smith's priority. He believed a good education to be the essential basis from which progress and prosperity would grow and built schools on all the main islands. As Lord Proprietor he imposed an inflexible rule that made attendance at school compulsory in the Scilly Isles some forty years before it became law in England. Parents had to pay towards the upkeep of the school: one penny a week if they attended and twopence if they did not!

Initially working closely with the SPCK who had first gone to Scilly in 1752, Augustus Smith made himself entirely responsible for all the island schools from 1840: he increased the salaries of the teachers, hired and fired them and provided up-to-date books and equipment for a good all-round education. For a century the islanders had scraped a poor living from fishing, kelp-making and smuggling; the Lord Proprietor's new rules stated that all children were to be trained to fit them for a trade. As the future of most boys would lie with the sea they studied navigation, and it was a proud Scillonian boast that all who went to sea from local schools rose to officer ranks, with many becoming ships masters.

The island schools are now administered by their own local education authority, but as it covers only one comprehensive school and four primaries, the Scilly Isles do not have their own advisory staff so have to rely on that of Cornwall – calling on them only when there are specific problems. Their isolation is not an absolute deterrent to Her Majesty's Inspectorate, but the often hazardous journey has obviously not been relished by some, as revealed by the long gaps between clusters of visits. For the Scillonians themselves there is no choice, their whole lives and way of life are governed by the sea which surrounds them. Since reorganisation in the mid-Sixties, off-island Secondary age children board weekly to attend the Isles of Scilly comprehensive school on St Mary's. Until then those who passed the 11-plus examination had a boarding school education in Cornwall and the rest stayed at their own island all-age school. Bryher lost its school in 1972 and its children have to make a journey by sea to school at Tresco every day.

The original Schoolhouse on St Martin's was built by the inhabitants themselves at a cost of £16, at a time when the islanders had neither carts nor wheelbarrows. Carrying the stones from the beach and cairns along the bridle-path in their arms, on their shoulders and in hand-barrows, the old granite schoolhouse commands such an

St Martin's School, Isles of Scilly, photographed at the turn of the century

incredibly stunning view of seascape that one schoolmistress had to paste brown paper over the windows to prevent her pupils being distracted by it!

The School, built to accommodate 72 – but averaging 30 pupils – was in the charge of Charles Culyer, who also taught Sunday School and was the parish clerk until after 1893. 'In quest of pastors and masters' took up much of Augustus Smith's time: 'my first object now is the catching of a schoolmaster to send down to Scilly forthwith ...' 'Old Caliban', as the islanders called their Lord Proprietor, relied on the mainland only for the training of teachers – he financed every aspect of Scillonian education. Only once did he miscast a teacher 'as he can't sing'.

The closely written lines of the unadorned Log Books conjure up their own illustrations of school life on an isolated island where the Headteacher has always been the only teacher. Mrs Heather Terry is the Head Teacher of St Martin's School where she, her father and grandfather were all pupils in their time. With a total population of some eighty on the whole island of St Martin's the activities of the school are a community concern so there is always strong support for whatever the school produces.

The problems which beset the small mainland villages – young couples unable to afford private property which is snapped up for retirement and holiday homes, and no council housing – also bedevil the small islands. But the smaller the scale the more magnified becomes the dilemma, and yet the village school is much the same wherever it is found. It is how it relates to the community and how the environment imposes its own characteristics on the school which makes each one so individually special. When your entire village is but a two-mile rock in the Atlantic every venture is an adventure.

21 Apr. 1941	The school was closed all day in order to enable the teacher to visit the dentist on St Mary's.
3 May 1943	Have received notice from LEA that the remainder of the Easter holidays is to be taken as an agricultural holiday, in order that the children may assist in the gathering of potatoes.
15 Dec. 1949	School closed to permit children to go to the main island of St Mary's for Christmas shopping.
29 Nov. 1954	Continuation of strong winds, registered 104 mph. Much damage to glasshouses and the few trees. Most of the children and parents have been up all night. Great quantities of seaweed on beaches. No mail for seven days.
24 Jan. 1955	Friday approx 9.10 p.m. *The Mando*, a Panamanian cargo boat wrecked. She struck the Golden Ball Bar during fog. Her tonnage: 10,000 tons.
25 Jan. 1955	Many islanders out wrecking.
20 Feb. 1957	Cable boat arrived from mainland. There is soon to be a new telephone system with underground cables.
10 Jan. 1968	Rather dry and cold for Scilly. A very good flower season.
18 Nov. 1978	Whale beached in Bread and Cheese Cove – found to be a Pilot Whale. Took photos for British Museum.
7 Dec. 1978	After attending a meeting on St Mary's, the Headteacher was stranded there for three days due to a severe S.E. gale.
15 July 1983	Tresco school came to St Martin's for a Treasure Hunt.
9 Sept. 1983	All the school children [the number on roll was at that time nine] with their mothers and friends went to St Mary's to be present at the live broadcast of Woman's Hour. Joanna Perkins read a piece about the flower season, which had been written by her brother Richard. Also, I spoke on island life and teaching in such a small school. We all enjoyed the experience and the children benefited from an explanation of technical details.
8 June 1984	St Martin's School children visited Round Island Lighthouse accompanied by their teacher and three fathers. This visit was arranged with Trinity House as part of this term's project about the sea, and obviously had to be undertaken on a calm day.

16 July 1984 — We attended St Martin's Auxiliary Coastguard drill near the island quay. The senior officer kindly allowed each child a ride in the Breeches Buoy rescue equipment. An interesting morning was followed by a swim in the sea and picnic lunch before afternoon school commenced. The islands dentist crossed by boat from St Mary's to inspect the pupils' teeth in the afternoon.

18 Feb. 1986 — School re-opened after the half-term break and we were switched on to mains electricity. The old diesel generator is at last redundant following the successful campaign which has resulted in the Scillonian off islands being connected to a mains supply.

Their remoteness did not totally isolate the islands from the disruptive rigours of the Second World War. Scilly became a base against hostile submarines, one of which was sunk and another wrecked and the little school became aware of being a part of Great Britain.

4 Sept. 1939 — Owing to the outbreak of hostilities between Great

The entire school of St Martin's await the boat that will take them on their annual school picnic, 1986

	Britain and Germany the school meetings have been abandoned until instructions to the contrary are received.
11 Sept. 1939	School re-opened this Monday morning. Roy Stevens aged 12 years has been re-admitted to this school for the duration of the war.
6 Sept. 1940	The men of the island have dug an air raid shelter for the use of the children in this school.
16 May 1941	In the carrying out of a test this afternoon in the wearing of gas masks, it was found that most of the children could wear them and work for a period of fifteen minutes without difficulty.

The personal interest of the island schools founder continued through the family with the Dorrien-Smiths signing the registers and bringing a tree and sweets from Tresco for St Martin's School Christmas parties until 1955, on the death of Major AA.

St Martin's School must now be the smallest in the British Isles. In 1977 there were but two pupils, that number has now doubled – thanks to the Headteacher having two daughters!

6 *The Past Presented for the Future*

THE PAST PRESERVED AND CONVERTED: NEW USES FOR OLD SCHOOLS

Entangled in the cobwebs of the schools ...

William Cowper

The old village school still lingers on in the memories of its former pupils. The thick stone walls, the height of the raftered roof; the panelled wainscot; the pot-bellied stove around which wet gloves and mufflers dangled on the fireguard, adding the pungent smell of toasted wool to mix with those of powdered ink, damp dry-rot, wax-polished timber, heady meadowsweet drying in pots, and jam jars of tadpole dotted murky water. Stirred together by the dynamic charge of dozens of warm, pulsating bodies weaving their own sharply sweet scents of quick dried socks, wet pants, plasticine-stained hands and cough-drop laden hot breath – the aura is as atmospheric as any graphic illustration; unique to school, embodied in its very fabric, the spirit of its children past that can never be quite eradicated.

Such is the atmosphere of the tiny village school at Sevington. Caught in a time-warp since it was last used before the Great War, it is a precious private place to which small school parties wind their way through the Wiltshire lanes to experience a little of schooldays past, without the formality of a public museum.

The old grey stone building with its steep roof and mullioned windows, which fascinated Thomas Hughes' Tom Brown, still stands on its 'angle of ground where three roads met'. After serving the village children of Uffington since James I was on the throne it is now a superb local museum. The table of rules laid down by its founder in 1617 is on the wall, and a wealth of material has been collected on the Hughes family; the museum is appropriately named 'Tom Brown's School'.

Captain Cook's old school in the High Street facing a waterfall is also a museum in his home village of Great Ayton in Yorkshire, where he spent most of his childhood. The family home was dismantled to be rebuilt in Australia.

Victorian schooldays hold a great fascination for today's pupils and provide ideal resource material for visiting school parties.

The Welsh Folk Museum at St Fagans, Cardiff, has a splendid single-room village school of 1880, re-erected from west Wales. A Schools Service Officer organises re-enactment of Victorian-style lessons with pupils who dress the part, and playground games of the period are also played.

Re-enacting the past is a vibrant aspect of today's curriculum. The famous Sweeps Procession at Rochester is a jolly affair far removed from the realities of the 'climbing boys' to whom St George the Martyr in London's Queen Square is popularly dedicated as 'the Sweep's Church', and Dickens portrayed so graphically in Mr Gamfield's breezy language: 'even if they're stuck in the chimbley, roasting their feet makes 'em struggle to hextricate theirselves'. More than a few boys, 'obsitnit' or not, get stuck today in the Victorian chimney at Sudbury Hall Museum of Childhood in Derbyshire for they are a lot better fed than the Oliver Twist thin children who were employed in this most dangerous and degrading form of child labour which did not end until 1875.

Heptonstall houses its past in the old grammar school in Churchyard Bottom of this village high on the Yorkshire moors, whereas Steyning in West Sussex turned theirs into a school library.

Grasmere gingerbread, made to the original village recipe, has been baked in the small school by the church lych-gate, having served the children of this 'loveliest spot that man hath ever found' – as Wordsworth described his Cumbrian home – from 1660 to 1854.

Teas are served in the former school, built by the Fitzherberts to commemorate Queen Victoria's Coronation in 1837, to the many visitors to Tissington. This lovely place with its broad verges and triangular village green is famous for its colourful well-dressings. Tissington is said to owe its salvation to the purity of its waters when the plague struck this part of Derbyshire, and the villagers still show their gratitude by creating beautiful pictures of flower petals around their five wells.

The Jacobean Grange at Grinshill sheltered in the Shropshire hills, is said to have been built for the children and teachers of Shrewsbury School as a retreat for whenever the plague struck in the seventeenth century.

The Green School at Barnes had a headmaster's house added to it in 1857. In 1926 the building was due to be demolished, but by a concerted effort by the local inhabitants it was saved and the old village school now serves as a Day Centre for Senior Citizens.

Avon's pretty Chew Magna held its first church-controlled school in the sixteenth-century Church Ale House from 1842 until the Board school was built in 1883. The Old Schoolroom near the church has

Hardy Amies chose an old village school for his country home

reverted to use for village functions. At Wyck Rissington, where Gustav Holst once lived on the village green, the school which the rector built at his own expense in 1848 on the glebe beside the church, became the Post Office.

Much sought after for conversion to private houses, the old schools of impressive solid structure are, on the whole, of outstanding architectural merit, evocative of the period. Hardy Amies, Britain's foremost designer and royal dressmaker chose an Oxfordshire village school for his country retreat, and grows lovely old-fashioned English roses in the playground. Between the heartsease and herbs, box-edged flower beds and symmetrical lines of sweet-smelling shrubs, his initials are spelt out among the cobblestones. The face it presents to the village street is still the same old stone schoolroom of 1860. Aesthetically and socially, where the schools have become village halls their function, though changed in emphasis, is still manifested in their original concept – that of serving the community as a focus of village life.

CELEBRATING A CENTURY: THE LIFE AND TIMES OF A VILLAGE SCHOOL THROUGH ITS LOG BOOKS

COATES VILLAGE SCHOOL, GLOUCESTERSHIRE 1849-1949

1849 Coates National School was built

1871

1871 First Log Book begun, prefaced by letter of HMI's visit carefully copied on to page 1

Education Department
30 Aug. 1871

Revd Sir,
I am directed to communicate to you, for the information of the Managers, the following copy of the report made by H.M. Inspector upon the occasion of his recent visit to your school.

The following are the results of the examination of the scholars according to the New Code

	Number presented	Number passed on Examination in Reading	Writing	Arithmetic
Boys, or mixed under Master	53	51	44	43
Girls, or maids under Mistress				

A family-sized school at Coates

This is a superior country school and has passed a fair examination under the New Code. It wants a little more apparatus for the Infants, a Log-book portfolio for official papers and some additional Registers.

F. R. Sandford

PS Mr Boucher's certificate under Article 59 will shortly be forwarded

(Mr and Mrs Boucher were the Master and Mistress, with the assistance of 4 unpaid monitors. 53 on roll.)

19 Aug.	Attendance very low this week owing to the Harvest having begun in the neighbourhood. Closed school for the Harvest holiday of 4 weeks.

1872

23 Mar.	Attendance low on Wednesday owing to the Duke of Beaufort's hounds assembling at the Ten-rides in Earl Bathurst's park. A boy has left for the plough, aged 10 years, just having acquired a knowledge of the simple rules of Arithmetic.
20 July	Attendance low owing to a Temperance Fete being held in Earl Bathurst's park.
27 July	Holiday for the Rector's Annual Treat.
28 Sept.	A bell has been erected on the roof of the school, kindly given by Mrs Cator of Trewsbury House.
9 Nov.	Three children absent the whole week – want of boots the cause.

1873

29 Mar.	A girl left school to nurse her mother's baby.
26 July	Holiday owing to a Fete when Blondin performed his extraordinary exploits on the high-rope in Earl Bathurst's park.

1874

12 June	A little girl has died, supposed through eating unripe gooseberries.
7 Aug.	Many children allowed leave by the Vicar to go gleaning.

1876

14 July	The Managers have provided lap-bags for the use of the scholars during their sewing lessons.
28 July	The parents being out in the fields at work, the children are kept at home to take care of the homes, or younger brothers or sisters.
4 Aug.	Through the kindness of A Cator Esq the scholars were taken to Cirencester to be present at a Wild Beast Show.

1878

20 Apr.	Usual visits made by the Rector who on one occasion examined the 1st class in Arithmetic.

1879

25 Apr.	Some few irregular scholars this week, the gardening having commenced.

1883

11 Oct.	The First Mop taking place on Monday and Wombold's Menagerie on Friday together with potato picking has caused irregularities this week.

1884

14 Mar.	Typhoid fever has appeared in the village.

1885

27 Feb.	A case of ringworm has occurred.

The character of the work, more especially in the Standard over which Mrs Ashman has direct charge is very high and in spite of some little inferiority of the Handwriting and Grammar of the Fifth Standard might entitle the school to the highest Merit Grant. It is, however, impossible to recommend this in view of the inferior style of the Needlework, which barely merited any Grant. Singing is not first rate.

HMI Report, 26 July 1886

1886

22 Dec.	The holidays are curtailed because so much time has been lost through illness.

1887

17 June — This Jubilee week has been somewhat a broken one owing to local festivities and Choral Festival in Cirencester.

The children should learn to speak out better when answering questions, and to moderate their shouts when reading. The use of fingers in calculating should also be discouraged. My Lords will look for improvement in the Needlework as a condition of a grant another year.

HMI Report, 15 Sept 1887

1888

25 May — Irregular attendance caused by bad weather we had no holiday this Whit week.

13 July — Because of scarlet fever in Tarlton the Managers think it advisable that no children should come from that village for a while.

This is on the whole, a good school, but there is imperfection of knowledge of the Repetition. This failing endangered the recommendation of the higher grant for English. In both rooms the Needlework exhibited was very dirty, and the test exercises were done in a slovenly manner. The Teacher under Article 84 would do better if she kept the children in smarter order by more precise school drill.

HMI Report, 11 Aug. 1888

1889

22 Feb. — Alice Smith has returned after an absence of 17 weeks through scarlet fever.

The HM Inspector states that in the Infant School the use of thimbles is not insisted on. They should be taught the use of thimbles from the very beginning. The right position of the needle cannot be secured unless a thimble is used.

HMI Report, 19 Aug. 1889

1890

25 Apr. — Another case of diphtheria has occurred, resulting in death.

Much good work is being done. Needlework is improved, but fixing is shown by the test exercises to need attention.

HMI Report, 21 Aug. 1890

1891

23 Jan.	Only 25 out of 68 children in school today. The coughing for some days has been quite distressing.
13 Feb.	It has been a pleasure to work in school this week as the attendance has improved.
18 Dec.	One third of the scholars absent from Influenza. I have been in bed, too, a good part of the week.

1892

19 Feb.	The progress of the Infants is not satisfactory, but with a village girl it is what might be expected.
19 Aug.	Today I resign my duties at this school after a period of 16½ years. Mrs Ashman, HT
5 Oct.	Mr R. T. Robinson commenced duties with Miss Wheeler as assistant.
21 Oct.	Found slight error in Infant Register and cautioned Miss Wheeler to be more careful in future.
23 Dec.	Miss Wheeler left.

1893

6 July	School Treat in honour of marriage between Prince George and Princess May. Holiday in afternoon.
4 Sept.	Miss Ellen May Bradshaw commenced duties in the Infant Room. Born in 1875.
3 Oct.	Miss Bradshaw having marked A Temple absent in error altered the mark to present. Spoke to her about the seriousness of such carelessness and told her to be more careful in future.

1894

18 June	Admitted three children from a barge on the Canal near Tunnel House. It is very evident from their attainments that they have not previously attended school.
15 Oct.	Closed the School for one week owing to the prevalence of measles. Every family in the village containing children having cases (except Williams and King).

Creditable pains have been again bestowed, as in former years, upon the religious work, and notwithstanding recent illness, with increased success.

HMI Report, 5 Dec. 1894

20 Dec.	The children gave Concert and Tableaux Vivants in the evening. Handed over £2 11s. 4d as the result. Miss

Bradshaw (who left on this date) presented with a watch and chain as a token of respect.

1895

7 May — Ben Roberts absent. Mother reports that probably another case of Typhoid.

8 May — Gave holiday till Monday in order to be free from any chance of danger on behalf of scholars while sanitary arrangements are being thoroughly overhauled and disinfected.

1896

1 Dec. — Had occasion to punish Ray Telling, as owing to Master's illness he thought it a rare opportunity to set all discipline at defiance, but was soon taught it to be a mistake.

1897

8 Aug. — Children wish to leave early to carry refreshments to parents in harvest field.

23 Sept. — Grant in aid of £10 has been made for the purpose of providing new desks.

1899

29 Mar. — Gave up charge of this school.

R. T. Robinson, HT

22 May — The work in some cases is carried on under disadvantages. The master having removed all text books, song books etc. they being his own property.

1900

2 Mar. — A half holiday is given on account of the Relief of Ladysmith.

9 Nov. — Notices from the Managers complaining of uncleanliness have been sent to the parents. One girl – Frances – was sent home for a fortnight as her head was in such a dirty state.

The room is very dull and would be much improved if the upper part of the partition were glazed and the walls coloured, and some good pictures procured. More ventilation is also needed.

HMI Report, 29 July 1901

1902

27 Mar.	Received several pictures and maps from Trewsbury House.
1 May	Girls have stayed away in the morning for washing day.
20 June	A week's holiday is given for the Coronation.

The rent of the Mistress' house to be £8 a year. A new larder to be built in the house. The Managers decided not to build a new bedroom on to Mrs Hunt's house as they considered that the size of the bedroom would not justify the spending of so much money.

Managers Meeting, 13 July 1904

1906

16 Feb.	Received 26 History books from Lady Bathurst for use in School.
2 Mar.	Gave a lesson on the threshing of corn. Children very delighted watching the process at a neighbouring farm.
23 Mar.	Mr Peel gave each child a packet of sweet peas to plant and tend in their home gardens.
25 May	Today given as holiday, but children assembled at 10 o'clock and were addressed by Major Balfour on the need of being good patriots and citizens. The patriotic song was sung and we marched to the Coronation Tree carrying the Union Jack where they sang God Save the King. We were joined by the Vicar, Major and Mrs Balfour, Mr and Mrs Peel and their children and governesses.
1 Aug.	The children's sweet peas grown by themselves were judged and Mr Peel gave four prizes 5/–.
21 Sept.	Susie Landridge having obtained a Scholarship, has left for Cirencester Grammar School.

The school to be known in future as the Coates Church of England School in place of the present name of Coates National School.

Managers Meeting, 6 Dec. 1906

1907

1 May	Received telegram from Dr Bond advising school closure immediately for 3 weeks as scarlet fever is in village.

Report made by HMI was read: 'the ventilation should be improved and the end windows of the Infants altered to admit more light and air'. Cesspits to be emptied. The Managers agreed to carry out the alterations but at the same time they thought they were quite unnecessary, the school being well lighted.

Managers Meeting, 10 Nov. 1907

1908

27 Apr.	The Assistant, Rose Eyles, was unable to return to school being snowed up at Bournemouth.
19 June	Took an object lesson on grasses. Children found several rare flowers by the side of the canal and many varieties of orchids.
9 Oct.	Received form regarding Medical Inspection to fill up.

1909

Canon Gibbs asked for the attendance of the children at Church on Ascension Day. This permission the Managers could not give. Canon Gibbs then wished that Mr Household might be written to on the matter.

Managers Meeting, 10 May 1909

23 June	Let children off to see the King pass on his way to Gloucester. Received medals to give to the children to commemorate the occasion.
22 Nov.	Received guards for fire-places.

1910

15 Apr.	Nurse Powell examined the children's heads.
22 Apr.	With proceeds of the children's concert in February and with contributions, a piano has been bought and received this week.
29 Apr.	Sent a wreath to the Shakespearean Festival from the school.

Rose Eyles having left attending the Church, the Managers wished to know if she was no longer a Member of the Church of England. Her secession would not qualify her to act as Teacher under the trust deed.

Managers Meeting, 4 June 1910

11 Nov.	Nurse Cotsworth gave Health Lecture, and will do every Friday.

The Dairywork Class is held in the Scullery Dairy of Mrs Swanwick's house. It is sufficiently large for the Class of 9 girls. It would be advantageous if a small bench could be placed so that the girls could sit while taking notes.

HMI Report, 21 Feb. 1911

1911

24 Mar.	Rose Eyles was presented with a silver watch and chain, as she leaves today owing to her father's death necessitating change.

31 May	There will be a week's holiday from 16 June to commemorate the Coronation, by the express wish of the King.
26 June	The children received Coronation Mugs.

1912

19 Apr.	Drew attention during the week to the terrible loss of the Titanic which went down 500 miles off the American coast. Noted the great benefit of Marconigram.
10 May	Frederick Reid being 7 years old, very troublesome at times, and although he has been at school 2 years can neither understand nor speak, but can imitate others.

1913

20 June	The infants use ink now and their work on the whole is neatly done.

The coal for the year to be supplied by the Kemble Co-operative Society. A letter was read from the Coates Parish Council in which they thought 2/6 was too much to be charged for fire, light and cleaning at each meeting. The Managers agreed in future to charge the Parish Council 1/6 a night.

Managers Meeting, 3 July 1913

4 July	Children are greatly interested in feeding the stickleback and in watching the tadpole developing.
17 Oct.	Took Infants for reading who are articulating better. There is still trouble with the dropping of the 'h'.
21 Nov.	Upper Class painting of hips and haws for Christmas cards.
19 Dec.	Dorothy Mustoe died of diphtheria four days after she left school.

1914

23 Jan.	The children's throats are still troublesome, am giving them 'Formalin'.
12 June	Took drill out of doors this week.
27 Nov.	Taught children National Anthem.

1915

26 Feb.	Admitted a boy who is very backward as his parents have had to remove four times lately owing to the war.
14 May	More flowers have been sent to our soldiers this week. Gave lesson on the bee. Took the boys into the garden to

watch the pollen brought in. Freda Roberts obtained 5/- prize from the Victoria League for an essay on 'Our Food Supplies from overseas and our dependence on it'.

21 May — Mr Burton called in and read his son's letters from the Trenches.

26 Nov. — Gave lesson on Thrift – have utilised small pieces of wool for knitting quilts to be sent to prisoners in Germany.

3 Dec. — Sent this week – 30 eggs for wounded.

1916

21 Feb. — The Mistress is obliged to be absent to attend Women's Agricultural War Meeting.

9 June — Jack Mustoe an old school boy is saved from the *Warrior*. He saw a German battle cruiser and two cruisers sunk and our own *Indefatigable* blown about 300 ft. into the air.

6 Oct. — Sent 4/- to Jack Cornwall Fund.

1917

28 Sept. — Nurse Woodliffe examined heads. The children have been digging potatoes this week every spare moment for the Hospital – sent 2½ cwt besides beet and cabbage. The boys have dug potatoes in place of Grammar.

11 Oct. — The children intend gathering chestnuts for munitions.

19 Oct. — Sent Henry Beal home because of his dirty habits. The Rector unable to take his regular Scripture lesson. Sent 6 cwts chestnuts for munition works.

7 Dec. — School Dinners began on Monday for the far-away children – the members of the Women's Institute taking it in turn to provide them for a week at a time.

1918

26 Apr. — Utilised the proceeds from garden produce in starting a School Library, also bought a football and a First Aid outfit.

3 May — Admitted 3 children who are in the district away from the raids in London.

7 June — Circulating library books were received today from Gloucester.

1 Nov. — One of the 'old' boys called and told the children his experiences in France during the Geography lesson.

15 Nov. — Heard the joyful news on Monday that the Armistice had been signed and that hostilities had ceased. Rang school-bell for an hour and let children have a long game of football. Miss Harrison gave a Peace Tea-Party to the children.

1919

Mrs Hunt stated that children admitted during the year have not been properly grounded and therefore she had put them back to work them up. One or two were mentally deficient and those that had been in the air raids were consequently nervous.

Managers Meeting, 25 July 1919

21 Nov.	Mrs Harrison called, drew her attention to the state of Percy Scriven's boots. Willie Tibbles has been troubled again with his eyes, although Mrs Harrison has provided him with a pair of goggles to wear in the cold winds.
19 Dec.	Frank Wilson had some spots which were rather suspicious.

1920

2 June	The afternoon was given as holiday owing to Women's Institute outing to Minchinhampton.
30 July	The Mistress was presented with a silver and cut glass smelling salt bottle on her retirement.
9 Nov.	The Managers have added a clause re Religious Instruction being held at 11 am on Red Letters Saints' Day so that the children may attend church.

1921

23 Mar.	The children's mothers were invited to come to school at 2.15 to see the children at work. Tea was provided by the Upper Division who had saved up pennies for the purpose.
10 May	The girls now have a netball court, the posts and balls were partly paid for by the proceeds of the school concert in December. The boys have a cricket pitch, with bats given by Mr Harrison. Children over 12 years are now allowed to join the Village Tennis Club.
1 Nov.	The children went to church it being All Saints Day.

1922

24 Mar.	Upper Class boys have formed a troop of Boy Scouts.
6 July	Children went home at 3.30 in consequence of the public enrolment of the Girl Guides.

A letter was read from the Education Secretary asking the consent of the Managers to re-organise the school as a Junior School – in consequence of the attendance having become very small.

Managers Meeting, 20 Sept. 1922

15 Nov.	School closed for General Election.

5 Dec.	The Attendance Officer told all children over 9 years of age that they will go to Cirencester School after Christmas.

1923

Miss Grace Davies commenced duties as Head Teacher. (Now a one teacher school)

12 Feb.	50 bundles of wood arrived.
16 Mar.	Received notice re vaccination on account of smallpox at Cheltenham.
26 Apr.	School closed today in honour of the Royal Wedding. The children brought decorations and had a tea in the school in the afternoon.
24 May	Empire Day. Lessons on the Empire. Half holiday. Children dressed up to represent countries of Empire, sang songs and saluted flag. Parents and friends invited. Had tea in school then went to the Women's Institute and sang Empire songs.

1924

1 Oct.	Dennis Tugwell and Gwendoline Roberts transferred to Cirencester schools.
10 Nov.	Penny Bank opened.

1925

16 Feb.	Took children to see sheep and lambs in field near.

A letter from the Education Authority was read as to the children who attended school certified not being properly fed. The Correspondent was instructed to write to the Education Authority and urge that the children should be fed in a suitable room and that they should eat their dinners under proper supervision, that they should be instructed to wash their hands before eating, and that facilities for making cocoa and heating milk should be provided.

Managers Meeting, 14 Oct. 1925

1926

Miss Davies asked for milk for 5 children on each school day, also a saucepan for heating the same and that the wash hand basin in the lobby should be repaired. It was decided not to provide milk as the Managers thought it was the duty of the parents to do so. Miss Cator undertook to see the parents of the children who have their mid-day meal in school and urge them to provide them with hot milk or Oxo. The Correspondent was instructed to write to chief residents in the parish asking for annual subscriptions, as was the custom until a few years back.

Managers Meeting, 1 Oct. 1926

1929

This school, which is now attended by younger children only, has 16 children on the books, 13 of whom are boys ... The old long backless desks make uncomfortable seats for these young children.

HMI Report, 14 May 1929

1933

Rev Simpson came with a letter from the Education Office suggesting that the fire be lit earlier in the winter mornings, as the temperature at 9 am was frequently 45°F or lower. He decided to ask the cleaner to light the fire at 7.30 am.

2 Oct.	2 ton 10 cwt coal arrived.

1934

26 Sept.	Allowed the children to hear the launch of the Queen Mary.
13 Oct.	Received notice about free milk.
9 Nov.	An invitation from Mrs Tabor to tea and a bonfire on Nov 29 on the occasion of the marriage of The Duke of Kent to Princess Marina.

The kindly and homely atmosphere created by the sympathetic treatment of the scholars suits the character and needs of the school.

HMI Report, 12 Dec. 1934

1935

3 May	School closed until May 8 in honour of His Majesty King George V's Silver Jubilee. All the children of the village (46) were entertained to tea at the school, each were presented with a mug, given by the British Legion and a Jubilee shilling by Major Daubney of Dockem House, who made a speech and read a telegram from His Majesty's Secretary thanking the children of Coates for their good wishes.

1936

28 Jan.	School closed for the funeral of King George V.

2 Mar. Mrs Nisbet of Thatched House has presented to the school a framed picture of King Edward VIII in Garter Robes.

1937

9 Mar. Mr and Miss Roberts, Post Office, have given a large doll and bedstead to the school.

23 Mar. Medical Inspection but Nurse Comer unable to be present so Head Teacher had to weigh and measure the children.

24 May Children had tea, sports and mugs in honour of the Coronation of King George VI and Queen Elizabeth.

It was resolved that 4 of the old desks be offered to the Cricket Committee for use as seats.

Managers Meeting, 28 Mar. 1938

1939

23 Mar. Handed over 4d, needlework receipts, to the Official Correspondent.

A proposal that the School be re-organised to take children up to 11 was found not feasible as the total number of 25 would not be sufficient to require two Teachers.

Managers Meeting, 27 Apr. 1939

14 July The Children presented Miss G M Davies with a letter attaché case, as a token of remembrance, on her leaving Coates for Cirencester.

11 Sept. Re-opened school one week late owing to evacuation of schoolchildren. Admitted 5 evacuated from West Ham. HMI Mr Tanner called this morning. Seating accommodation insufficient.

10 Dec. 5 cwt of coal delivered for use of the evacuees during holidays.

1940

18 Jan. The highest temperature recorded in the schoolroom for the past 10 weeks has been 46°F.

It was reported that no grant for the (school lavatory) repairs would be forthcoming from the Education Committee, but that the Diocesan Council of Education, promised a small sum and a grant from Church funds would be made towards the cost of these repairs.

Managers Meeting, 26 Jan. 1940

29 Mar.	The coal supply has been used up. But very low temperatures make some heat in the school necessary.
15 July	The County Surveyor called to see what arrangements could be made in case of air raids during school hours. It was decided to protect the windows of the classroom with wire netting.
1 Oct.	The children are now listening to, and taking part in Wireless Broadcasts.
19 Nov.	Received 19s 0½d from the Forestry Commission for the beach nuts and acorns collected by children. 10/- of this went to the children and 9s 0½d was put into the fund for buying wool for army, navy and air force scarves.

1941

26 Feb.	Six of the older children are buying recorders and we have formed a recorder band.
31 Mar.	A new grate was fitted in the school. The children now *all* bring their gas masks and practise wearing them. The following broadcast lessons have been followed fairly regularly this term – Music and Movement History Story Travel Talk The Music Shop Let's Join In (Junior English) The children at first seemed unable to follow very much of what was said in these lessons, but their 'listening' power improved very rapidly and now only 3 of the most backward children find any difficulty in following the lessons.
8 May	14 children have planted school gardens.
25 June	Took older children to swimming bath.
23 Dec.	Children went carol singing and collected £3 10s for Mrs Churchill's Aid to Russia Fund.

This is quite a remarkable school. The Headmistress has an unusual gift for teaching and so the children are really interested and learn quickly and thoroughly. Original methods are used with great success; for instance the children have painted scenes from the life of St Francis of Assissi which are pasted together and placed on a roller. Prayers are also most helpful and the tone is excellent.

Diocesan Inspector's Report, 24 Mar. 1942

1942

31July	Parents Day. Parents were invited to see the work done during the year. Puppets and recorder playing were

given. The exhibits included a model of Coates village made by the three oldest boys out of match boxes. Plain sewing prizes were won by Kathleen Rebbett and Mary Auden, and an attendance prize won by Irene Mander. Major Daubney offered to give a prize next year for good manners.

22 Sept. 115 lb of rose hips collected.

6 Oct. I (L.A. Simpson, supply teacher) have arranged to use the school bicycle for my journey to and from Cirencester.

13 Oct. Mr Butt, a local farmer, sent for John Hovard and John Smith to help potato picking.

15 Dec. Major Daubney came in to warn the children of the dangers of the new types of incendiary and other bombs.

1943

29 Mar. All children sent home after prayers so that Kathleen Rebbett could take the scholarship examination.

25 May Mr Burdon (Inspector of Schools to LCC) called to see the accommodation available. Furniture will be arriving shortly to equip the spare classroom which is to be used by the Junior children who are at the convalescent home in the village.

The Deputy Secretary to the Education Committee attended to put before the Managers a proposal that the outer School room should be used for a class of LCC children now living at Dockem House. The children were under the auspices of the Red Cross but as they came from London the LCC had been approached to provide Teachers and equipment for their education. It was finally decided that the room would be let to them 'provided that they (the Managers) are not put to any expense'.

Managers Meeting, 1 June 1943

20 July Loaned 8 inkwells (2 new safety ones) to the evacuee class at Dockem House.

1944

15 Feb. Mr Walter called. I handed over the money and coupons for 6 pairs of wellingtons (30/-).

28 July Prize day – prizes included Jean Miles and Maurice Tibbles (courtesy prizes) Irene Mander for a year's perfect attendance.

1945

The builders had mended the school house door but would not undertake the chimney. The Chairman gave a resume of the (Education) Bill particularly with regard to its provision for Church Schools, pointing out the difference between the school becoming a Voluntary 'Controlled' or 'Aided' School. The vital importance of maintaining our school where religion could be taught according to the tenets of the Church of England. For an 'Aided' School the Government would provide 50% towards cost of reconstruction, also whole cost of the provision of Playing fields and upkeep of playground, and half the cost of future repairs. The Managers would be responsible for finding the remainder, but both the National Society and the Diocese would have funds available. Little could be done until the LEA had made known their plans, but we must be prepared to raise the funds necessary when the time comes. The Managers strongly expressed their determination to retain the School if this was at all possible.

Managers Meeting, 19 Jan. 1945

6 Feb	Loaned 15 reading books to Sapperton School. Reported overflow pipe to the Rector.

A really admirable village school –

Diocesan Report, 11 June 1945

29 June	Received 2 blackboards, 1 easel and 8 pegs.
6 Sept.	Rector took Scripture and Mr Jackson repaired leakage in girls' lavatory.
13 Sept.	Mr Walter brought a cyclostyle on loan from the Council school.
8 Oct.	Half day for the Mop.

The Chairman read the plan of the LEA for the proposed closure of the School. After careful consideration the Managers expressed strong disapproval and the view that every effort should be made to retain the school.

Managers Meeting, 4 Dec. 1945

1946

The Rev Gilpin, Director of Religious Education and Diocesan Inspector of Schools was present in order to explain the situation with regard to the Education Act 1944, the proposed closure of the School by the LEA and to give advice as to the next step to be taken by the Managers. He made it clear that the only question at the moment was the retention of the School and the question of raising money or as to the School being 'Aided' or 'Controlled' did not arise at this stage. The case for the retention of the School must now be sent to the Minister of Education direct who had issued new instructions that each village school must and would be considered on its own merit. Mr Gilpin commended the protest already sent to the LEA by the Managers … Mr Gilpin made the following points. The Minister of Education would consider: 1. Parents' wishes. 2. Feasibility of Transport. 3. Contribution to Village Life. 4. Procurability of land to bring the School up to the required standard. The numbers in the school would not take precedence. Mrs Swanwick suggested adding to the fact of there being an excellent school house, which was felt to be a valuable and wise suggestion and was agreed. The Minute of 4 December 1945 was reaffirmed, proposed by Mrs Payne and seconded by Mr Tugwell.

Managers Meeting, 9 May 1946

11 Nov.	Two student teachers from Cheltenham Ladies College came to this school for one month's practical training. They are Miss Morgan and Miss Gibbon.
22 Nov.	Received 19 pairs P T plimsolls and 57 pairs shoelaces.

1947

Received a communication that no school could be re-decorated at present unless it had not been done for the past 12 years. With the assistance of the LEA and Mrs Swanwick a wireless had been procured for the school.

Managers Meeting, 28 Feb. 1947

20 Apr.	Sent the school bicycle to the Girls Council School.
6 May	Mr Walters took the cyclostyle back to the Boys Council School.
27 Nov.	The builders came and started removing coal for building the school canteen.
8 Dec.	One large cook's table arrived.

1948

30 Jan.	Water laid on in the school. Two washbasins put in the cloakroom. Water is also laid on in the canteen. The water from the two washbasins runs into the drain in front of the kitchen window of the school house. Mr Thompson, the county architect came to look at this drain, and today I checked the canteen items.
9 Feb.	Visit of Air Vice Field Marshal Cassidy about erecting a barrier outside the school and also a 'School' sign in the village.
16 Mar.	One electric pole put in my garden with wires attached to the school, and an electric meter placed in canteen pantry. Received one smothering cloth, fire extinguisher and one doormat.

1949

19 Jan.	School canteen opened successfully with 11 children staying.
26 July	Today was prize-giving day. The Rev Sutton was in the chair and reminded those present that this year was the School's Centenary. Parents looked at the paintings, needlework and the children's gardens.

The last assembly. Coates School closed in 1987 with six pupils

The Chairman outlined the position as to the playground. It was thought better not to proceed with the matter. No decision had been transmitted to the Chairman as to the closure of the School it was thought by the Diocesan Council of Education that the position would be known early in 1950.

Managers Meeting, 5 Sept. 1949

1987: MOVE TO SAVE SCHOOL FAILS

A last ditch attempt by residents of Coates to save their village school from closure has failed.

Secretary of State for Education, Mr Kenneth Baker, has approved the recommendation by Gloucestershire County Council that the school should close this summer. He announced his decision only hours after meeting a three-man delegation from Coates who put the case for 'mothballing' the school for two years, during which time the number of primary school age children is expected to increase ... Coates had 14 children of primary school age and 26 not yet at school, and there were plans for 50 new houses in the village in the near future ... The school closed with just 7 pupils on the roll.

Wilts and Gloucestershire Standard: 14 Aug. 1987

OUR VILLAGE HERITAGE: POLICY, PLANS AND PROSPECTS

'I like village schools', said Mrs Margaret Thatcher. So why is it that with the Prime Minister making such a bold statement in a BBC Election Call programme in 1983 so many – over 1,000 rural schools since the mid-sixties – have closed, with reviews on the future of as many again? Taking the children from the village scene to be transported miles away to make up a supposedly economically composed unit is the crucial blow which cracks the rural community to become a 'desirable residential area' – but no longer a living village.

It is neither nostalgia nor sentimentality that keeps the question close to the heart of villagers throughout our green and pleasant land. It *is* the heart. The village school is the heart of the village community. No other slice of our social history has been so vital to the whole. Few other local issues generate so much heat and passion: headlines scream across the papers – Rural decay must stop – Village schools need special treatment – Axe will fall unless – Labour plea on village schools – and yet, over the past decade they are picked off, school by school, at an average rate of one every five days.

Schools often bring people to live in the neighbourhood; a village without a school will not attract young families, and without the continuity of generations the village dies as a community. Villages today have become an estate agent's happy hunting ground: peaceful, rural – the adjectives come easily; the advertisements extol the easy accessibility to the motorway to lure the city-weekender down to it and ramble on to reach the nest-egg of the recently retired – but do they ever mention the village school?

With the demise of the old squire and the consequent break up of the manorial social order, few villages have the patriarchal force which once knit them close. One village which has been saved for its villagers is Guiting Power, a Cotswold stone-built pocket around an agricultural estate – 'a family village' strengthened and sustained by the formation of a charitable Trust to ensure local people can live in their home parish, with a village school serving their educational needs.

The sad fact remains that so often the threatened closure of a village school is accelerated by the villagers themselves. At the very rumblings of a rumour some parents look for alternative larger schools rather than give the small village school the support which is so vital to it. By questioning its viability they start sounding its death knell, the fight for survival then becomes the harder for the few.

The few do make it on occasion, however. Getting something done at local level depends on setting it in the national scene – knowing what is being done in the county and in the country, and getting in quickly with resolution and resources.

A whole new network of organizations aimed at looking at rural social issues and backing community initiatives is both indicative of the real size of the many problems facing the village today, and the hope for solving them. The two major action associations concerned with small village schools are ACRE – Action with Communities in Rural England, a unique new charity launched in 1987, controlled by its member Rural Community Councils who also provide most of its funds – and NASSS – National Association for the Support of Small Schools.

NASSS was born in Onecote, a village in the Staffordshire Moorlands, when groups from Cumbria, Norfolk and Staffordshire had come together in 1978, fighting to save their village schools and decided to form a national organisation. Communities should prepare well in advance. Too many action groups come to us for help and expertise far too late. Parents do not fight for inferior schools. They fight because village schools have educational and social advantages which are too precious to lose.

National Association for the Support of Small Schools

In order to close, or implement any other major changes in schools, the Local Education is required under Section 12-16 of the Education Act 1980 to publish proposals and submit a copy to the Secretary of State. These proposals have to be published for a statutory period of two months, during which time any ten or more local government electors, governors of any voluntary school affected, and any other Local Education Authority concerned, may submit an objection to the proposals to the Local Education Authority. At the end of the two-month period copies of any objections made, found not withdrawn in writing, must be submitted together with the Authority's observations on them to the Secretary of State.

Department of Education and Science

The procedures involved are fairly complex and vary between Local Education Authorities, but a basic pattern is:
Rural/Small school policy – closure proposal – Area advisory committee – consultation with Managers, teachers, parents, community – Schools/Education development sub-committee – Education Committee – Full Council – Public notice – objections – Approval/Rejection by Secretary of State.
The crucial period for campaign groups is from when a proposal is made public to when closure is formally approved by the Education Committee (or possibly full Council).

National Council for Voluntary Organisations

If the Departments think, as they apparently do think, that palatial schools are desirable in country districts they will have to build themselves and take the consequences. But if they are prepared to treat rural education in a reasonable way there need, in my view, be no such great public expenditure.

Chairman of Managers, Abinger Hammer, 1907

In the case of Abinger Hammer those words still ring true eight decades on, for it incurs no national public expense. Since 1944 the future of the village school had come under scrutiny: first rumblings came when 'distance of the children's homes from other schools' was investigated; then an imposition in 1975 of a 'catchment' rule about transport to Middle Schools to which Abinger lost its 8-11 year olds some four years previously, made the decline in school numbers artificially accentuated; and the County Council issued its closure notice when the school roll fell to twelve in January 1982.

Vigorous campaigning against the closure achieved no change of Council heart, but strengthened the resolve of the villagers to keep the school at the heart of their community. The sense of continuity of great-grandchildren attending the village school of their youth brought support from the older generation as well as the parents who believed so utterly that small children should start their school career as close to home as possible; that happiness and security in those early years provide the basis for a happy and responsible adult life.

Abinger Hammer was fully aware of how much diminished a village is after losing its school – the vital point of contact and support of families who cherish and value the wider loyalties which are nurtured in belonging to a small community. Such tenacity to traditional values, energetic fund-raising, self-help and a clearly defined policy turned a novel and bold venture into a model example of how much can be achieved by so few for so many – and Abinger Hammer Village School Trust has now realised its aims and objectives, since opening as a non-fee-paying First School in the autumn term of 1982 following the County's closure of it at the end of the Summer term.

As a charitable trust, under a Board of Governors and with the support of patrons, the school is rented from the landlords, heirs of the Farrer family who built it in 1873. Financed from the income of a capital raised by deed of covenant, donations and fund-raising events, the First School (on which the 5-8 year olds of the village itself has first claim) is non-fee-paying. A fee-paying nursery department, catering for 3-5 year olds, is run in part of the school building, and extra-mural adult classes and courses add to the income and make full use of the building during evenings and holiday periods.

A fully-qualified teacher and specialists for different subjects are employed by the Trust. Parents and friends of the school help out with ancillary services and the whole community is involved with the wide social programme and fund-raising.

The Abinger Hammer School Trust's target remains unchanged: to build up an endowment that will secure the village school for ever – the trusting aim of the early founders of village schools throughout the kingdom.

The old school at Little Comberton now serves as a village hall

Similar schemes have been set up in various parts of the country by enterprising groups who value the flexibility, integration and unity of the village school. A national Movement for Education on a Human Scale has been launched by the Schumacher Society to lobby the government to fund parent-teacher initiated small schools. The Small School, established in 1982 in the North Devon village of Hartland, provides secondary school education within the local community – an act of faith demonstrating that 'Small is beautiful' in the field of education and that villages should, and can, have their own schools at their very heart.

Parent involvement has increased dramatically over the years. Early Log Books speak of visits from belligerent parents mainly opposed to the system and its implementation. Today, the skills and talents, time and interest of the parents are encouraged and directed to integrate with and support the teaching team, from transporting pupils to swimming baths to helping with cookery lessons.

At Barkby, parents are invited to attend a weekly Assembly, followed by coffee with the staff. This allows for brief informal contact – invaluable for a school where every teacher is fully committed to a time-table, with no free periods whatsoever, and, as at other schools, there are also Open Evenings.

The village school has long been the community centre in many rural areas, and this facility is a weighty argument for retaining the school.

On Night School nights the big fire grates were stacked up with coal in both the Infants and big schoolroom after the school children had left, so that by the time the school opened at 6 o'clock it was warm and the rooms were illuminated by 50 candle power paraffin lamps. Lessons were from 7 to 9 p.m., but the school remained open until 10 o'clock. The hour before and after lessons was a substitute for today's Youth Clubs, when suitable games were played and many people just sat around the fires and gossiped in the warm and well-lighted atmosphere.

Bert Amos, Drayton Parslow, Bucks.

Some twenty local education authorities now have designated community schools – including some village schools. The first community centre based on a village primary school in Leicestershire is at St Hardulph's School at Breedon on the Hill, famous for its church with the Saxon angel. The concept of community schools is not new, they have been linking the schools with their communities – their purpose – for some sixty years in smaller or lesser degrees and are designed to be more than opening up for the village band practice nights.

NASSS advises the retention of the schools' own governing body, its own instruments and articles of Government to meet the definition of 'school'. Flexi-schooling with open-learning techniques is the life-line that has kept the village school at Ticknall in Derbyshire – Britain's first 'flexi-school', owned by an educational trust.

Experiments in 'Cluster' or 'Federation' groupings of small schools have found favour in some rural communities. In this way specialist teachers and resources are shared – as in the Small Schools Project, initiated in 1982 and operated with enthusiasm at Besthorpe in Nottinghamshire. Grouping of Schools under one Head Teacher is already practised by some counties, and was introduced as an experiment in 1979 in Northumberland's Harbottle School. In this way two small schools were saved from closure. The 'experiment' is still running with teachers shared between the two schools, the older pupils of both schools brought together on a regular basis, thus increasing the peer grouping, and many functions and outings run jointly.

'The idea that 10,000 schools and numerous volunteer community groups can between them, and in conjunction with the BBC, complete a survey of modern Britain to mark the 900th Anniversary of King William's 1086 Domesday Survey, is so crazy it is bound to succeed ... The Project has been tried out in 17 schools throughout Britain, and I myself piloted it in a small two-teacher village school at Clyst St George in Devon ... The Domesday

Project offers a unique opportunity to be part of one of the most remarkable examples of collaboration in the twentieth century which has aroused not only national but considerable international interest. I thoroughly enjoyed working with the children at Clyst St George ...'

Professor E. C. Wragg

That Professor Wragg, Director of the School of Education of University of Exeter, should choose a small village school in which to pilot the most monumental and educational undertaking in modern history is proof enough of the importance of the village school in our society today. That he also piloted the BBC's Junior Micro-Electronics Course at the same village school is testimony to the progressive vitality in such small schools.

Those who teach in village schools are able and ready to demonstrate how high standards can be achieved with smaller numbers and how the curriculum can be richer than that of larger schools. On two consecutive years, Lynsted and Norton proved to be one of the best thirty schools in the country's literary world when the small school won awards in the W H Smith Young Writers Competition. To produce anything in a small school the demands are greater on the few and it is this high level of participation that instils responsibility and pride in the individual, a sense of belonging and the part he or she plays

The last moments of the village school at Daglingworth as it closed with only eight pupils in 1986

in the complex order of society – a social circle in which he or she knows and is known, respects and is respected.

Statistics have proved that the village school child is also a greater respecter of property than his urban cousin, so real costs of maintenance are a considerable factor when assessing the economics of educating a rural population – weighed also against the ever-increasing expense of transporting children to the towns. Economies of heating and lighting are easier to control in family size units; economising and improvising on materials and resources come more naturally to country folk and stretches both the budget and individual initiatives. But the true values are the intangibles, worth immeasurable by cost; the impalpable sense of belonging, of parochial pride; security and happiness born of stability and continuity – roots from which our very heritage has grown. To harvest or lay waste – the choice is ours.

Whilst writing this book I shared the final hours with the teachers and children of two local village schools as they closed after long and honourable educational service to the families of Daglingworth and Coates. With dignity and devoid of drama, they assembled to the clanging tone of the old school bell high in its arched tower, and

Playtime at Sapperton

gathered round their kind-faced Headteacher at the piano. As she played the plangent notes the thin little voices raised the old familiar songs of praise to the lofty beams:

Morning has broken
Like the first morning …

But it wasn't the first morning – it was the last afternoon. And soon they were gone. Clutching their farewell gifts, promises to teacher that they would be good at their new school and remember the happy times here at their old school still on their lips, they tumbled across the hopscotch patch in the playground and swung on the wicket gate as their Mums and Grand-dads and Great-Aunts had done before disappearing down the tree-shaded lane; their heads bobbing out of sight before their voices were out of sound. The void they left was as if they had never been.

A happier visit was to the third of the villages' triangle. Sapperton School set in its Cotswold Valley had just caught the attention of the national press and television for its enterprising publication of *Village Heritage*. Flushed with the sudden fame and fun of it all, one of the little co-authors caught my hand: 'We are only small, but they won't close our school now,' he confided confidently, 'not now we've done our book.'

Sources

In addition to the individual log books, managers' minutes and HM Inspectors' Reports of many schools, the main sources of my research have been Education Acts and By-laws and the following published works, which I acknowledge with gratitude.

NASSS Information Sheets

Headmaster and pupils, *A Walk through Hanmer*

Barney, Patrick, (compiled by) *Stelling Minnis and Upper Hardres*

Beresford, Maurice, *The Lost Villages of England*

Bridgman, Phil, *Cotswold Chronicle*

Corben, P.J., *Hemington School*

Crofts, P.H., and Lewis, D.C., *A History of Netherton C. of E. School*

Hadfield, Alice Mary, *The Chartist Land Company*

Harwood, J.S., *Songs of the Vale* (compiled by) Jeacock, Edith (courtesy of John E. Little), *History of Uffington School*

Nightingale, Florence, *Notes on Nursing* (1859)

Pender, Sid, *Thesis on Education on Isles of Scilly*

Perrins, Wesley, *Early Education in the Lye and Wollescote*

Roberts, Alun, *Hanes Ysgolion Borthygest a Morfa Bychan*

Shaw, Robin, *Dodford, 100 years in the Life of a Village School*

Swinford, George, Judith Fay and Richard Martin, *The Jubilee Boy*

Whitworth, W., *Crabbe Street School*

Willetts, Cliff, *When I was a Boy*

Witt, Stanley, *Gorsley Goff's School*

——————, *A School to Remember*

Yardley, Stanley George, *Wordsley, Kingswinford: The Recorded History of a School.*

Index

Page numbers in bold type refer to illustrations